Burt Franklin: Research & Source Works Series 250
Selected Essays in History Economics & Social Science 64

THE RISE OF THE LONDON
MONEY MARKET : 1640–1826

THE
RISE OF THE LONDON
MONEY MARKET
1640–1826

BY

W. R. BISSCHOP

WITH A PREFACE BY H. S. FOXWELL

Burt Franklin: Research & Source Works Series 250
Selected Essays in History Economics & Social Science 64

Burt Franklin
New York, N. Y.

Published By
BURT FRANKLIN
235 East 44th Street
New York, N. Y.   10017

ORIGINALLY PUBLISHED
LONDON: 1910

Reprinted 1967

This work has been reprinted
on long-life paper

Library of Congress Catalog Card No.: 68-56765

Printed in U.S.A.

INTRODUCTION

DR. BISSCHOP'S *The Rise of the London Money Market,* 1640 *to* 1826, now for the first time translated into English, first appeared, in the original Dutch, at the Hague in 1896. It was at my request that Dr. Bisschop very kindly undertook to have the work translated, and I willingly comply with his suggestion that I should write a few lines by way of preface.

Those who have worked at the history of English banking well know that the special chapter of that history which Dr. Bisschop has attacked is the most obscure and difficult of all, and has hardly been attempted by previous writers. Every historian has felt bound to give some account of the origin of our English deposit-banking, and hence every history has something to say about the Goldsmith bankers. But it is surprising how little definite knowledge we have of the business done by these men, and the very date at which they commenced operations is still uncertain. The Bank of England, after its foundation, seems to have monopolised the attention of the historian ; and the parallel development of private banking has been left in the shade, to be treated mainly by local antiquaries and others, whose interests were rather personal than economic. In general histories we hear little of country banking until we come to the period of the Restriction.

For the Bank of England we now have, thanks to Professor Andréadès, a fairly connected history, from its foundation to the present time. But even in regard to the Bank our knowledge is very defective, so far as concerns its actual methods of business and the nature of the instruments by which the business was carried on. Its statistical history is almost a complete blank for three-quarters of a century. There are no published returns of any authority until we come down to those arising out of the Committees towards the close of the eighteenth century, and these do not in general go back farther than

1778. For reasons difficult to understand, and in striking contrast to the practice of some other great national banks, the Bank of England has shrouded its operations in a veil of mystery, only penetrable by parliamentary inquiry. We are thus deprived of what would have been the natural clue to the history of a banking system in which the national bank has always been the predominant partner.

Of late years, no doubt, we have had some very valuable contributions to our knowledge of the dark ages of English banking. Among these I would mention especially the works of Mr. Maberly Phillips on the Northumberland and Durham banks, of Mr. Cave on the Bristol banks, and of Mr. Hilton Price and the late Mr. J. B. Martin on the London banks. What little we know about seventeenth and eighteenth-century banking is mainly due to these writers. In none of these works, however, do we find such a continuous history of banking operations and banking accounts as Mr. Boase has given us for Scotland in his history of the Bank of Dundee. It would be a great addition to our material for English banking history if we could have a reasoned and documented account of one or two English provincial and City banks over the period treated by Mr. Boase. All the books just mentioned, though full of matter for which students must be grateful, deal very largely, no doubt for sufficient reasons, with personal, biographical, and often merely humouristic details.

Thus it happens that the history, of English banking before the nineteenth century is little more than a disconnected series of episodical sketches, dealing with incidents of runs, forgeries, and crises, and diversified with vignettes of eccentric financiers, and stories of their whims, foibles, and fortunes. In fact, we know little more of English private banking for the seventy-five years after the foundation of the Bank than we do of the Goldsmith banking for the fifty years before that event—and not a great deal more about the Bank itself after the early struggles which established its monopoly. We have no figures for any English banks, giving information as to turnover, reserves, and rates, over any period of years ; such casual facts as can be gleaned are mostly to be found scattered in the works of the authors named. This statistical history, one must hope, will some day be forthcoming—at least, in the case of the national bank, whose accounts would be of the greatest historical value. But apart from statistics, we still lack, what is perhaps even more essential, a clear and scientific description of the gradual development of banking operations, and of the precise forms of the instruments by which these operations were conducted.

It is here, in the analysis of the growth of English banking business and English banking documents, that I believe Dr. Bisschop's work will be found most valuable. I do not know where else, in the whole literature of English banking history, we can find such a close, continuous, and reasoned study of English banking business before the rise of the joint stock banks. Dr. Bisschop has known how to make use of the scanty and scattered material already published : and it will be apparent to the careful reader that he has had the good fortune to enjoy very special facilities, facilities never before accorded, so far as I know, to any historian of

English banking. He has made such good use of them that one cannot but regret that they were not more freely extended. It is now beyond question that material exists which, if it could be examined by competent persons, would go far to fill the discreditable gaps in our knowledge of the history of the world-famous banking system of Great Britain.

In any case, Dr. Bisschop has made the most of what was available. More especially he seems to me to have thrown quite new light upon the evolution of the cheque system. Every one knows that this is the characteristic feature of English banking ; and yet it is not too much to say that there is nothing more obscure than the early history of cheque banking, and the precise reasons which led to its predominance in this country. Ignorant as I unfortunately am of the Dutch language, it was clear to me that Dr. Bisschop's book had broken new ground in this direction ; and it was my sense of the importance of this part of his work that led me to ask him to allow it to be translated.

I wish to take this opportunity of expressing my obligation to Dr. Bisschop for not only granting my request, but very kindly undertaking himself to have the translation made. I am sure that all those who are interested in the history of English banking will share my gratitude.

H. S. FOXWELL.

CAMBRIDGE, *October*, 1910.

TABLE OF CONTENTS

CONTENTS 15

PAGE

CONTENTS 15

PAGE

CONTENTS   15

PAGE

LIST OF WORKS QUOTED

Bagehot, W. : "Lombard Street," a description of the money market. London, 1908. New and revised edition, with notes by E. Johnstone.

Boase, C. W. : "A Century of Banking in Dundee." Edinburgh, 1867.

Bankers' Magazine. London. (Monthly.)

Child, Sir Josiah : "New Discourse of Trade." London, 1694-8.

Craddocke, Francis : "An Expedient for Taking Away All Impositions, and Raising a Revenue Without Taxes." London, 1661.

Cunningham, W. : "The Growth of English Industry and Commerce." Cambridge, 1890-2. Two volumes.

Fullarton : "On the Regulation of Currencies." London, 1844.

Gilbart, W. J. : "The History, Principles, and Practice of Banking." New Edition, revised by Ernest Sykes, B.A. Oxon. London, 1907.

Goldschmidt, Dr. L. : "Handbuch des Handelsrechts." Third Edition. Vol. I. : Universalgeschichte des Handelsrechts. Stuttgart, 1891.

Hermitage, N. de l' : "Secret Correspondence with the States General of the Netherlands, 1694 and following years." MS. in the British Museum.

Juglar, Clément : "Des Crises Commerciales et de leur retour périodique en France, en Angleterre et aux États-Unis." Paris, 1889. Second edition.

Kerr, A. W. : "History of Banking in Scotland." Glasgow, 1884.

Lawson, W. J. : "The History of Banking." London, 1855.

Luttrell : "A Brief Relation of State Affairs." Oxford University Press. Six volumes.

Macaulay, Th. B. : "The History of England from the Accession of James the Second." London, 1855. Five volumes.

MacLeod, H. Dunning : "Dictionary of Political Economy." Vol. I. London, 1863.

MacLeod, H. Dunning : " The Theory and Practice of Banking." London, 1883.

—— " The Theory of Credit." London, 1889-91.

Macpherson, D. : " Annals of Commerce, Manufactures, Fisheries, and Navigation." London, 1805. Four volumes.

Malynes, G. de : " A Treatise of the Canker of England's Commonwealth." London, 1601.

Martin, Frederick : " Stories of Banks and Bankers." London, 1865.

Martin, J. Biddulph : " The Grasshopper in Lombard Street." London, 1892.

Mees, W. C. : " Proeve eener Geschiedenis van het Bankwezen in Nederland." Rotterdam, 1838.

Pepys, Samuel : " Diary and Correspondence of S. P." London, 1854. Four volumes.

Philippsberg, Dr. Phillipovich von : "Die Bank von England im Dienste der Finanzverwaltung des Staates." Wien, 1885.

Phillips, Maberly : " History of Banks, Bankers, and Banking in Northumberland," &c. London, 1894.

Pierson, N. G. : " Leerboek der Staathuishoudkunde." Haarlem, 1884-90. Two volumes.

Price, F. G. Hilton : " Ye Marygold."
London.

—— " Handbook of London Bankers." London, 1876.

—— " The Signs of Old Lombard Street." London.

Ray, George : " The Country Banker." London, 1885.

Rogers, J. E. Thorold : " The First Nine Years of the Bank of England." Oxford, 1887.

Smith, Adam : " An Inquiry into the Nature and Causes of the Wealth of Nations." London, 1812. Three volumes.

Struck, Dr. Emil : " Skizze des Englischen Geldmarktes," in G. Schmoller's " Jahrbücher für Gesetzgebung, Verwaltung und Volkswirtschaft im Deutschen Reich." Leipzig, 1886-7.

Thornton, Henry : " Enquiry into the Nature and Effects of Paper Credit." London, 1802.

Tooke, Th. : " A History of Prices and of the State of the Circulation from 1793 to 1847." London, 1838-48. Four volumes.

" Zeitschrift für das Gesammte Handelsrecht." Edited by Dr. L. Goldschmidt. Stuttgart, 1858.

" A Brief Account of the Intended Bank of
England." London.

" A History of the Bank of England." London, 1797.

" Mystery of the Newfashioned Goldsmiths or
Brokers." Reprinted in J. B. Martin's
" The Grasshopper in Lombard Street."

AUTHOR'S NOTE

THERE is little to be added to the Preface which I wrote to this volume when it first appeared in Holland. The bankers who—when this work was in preparation—tendered me their kind assistance have all passed away. Whether they have been succeeded by a generation which is equally eager to bring to light all the historical treasures hidden in the storerooms of London and country banks, I do not know. A few applications which I did make for admission to those records did not meet with the desired success. I daresay, however, that my appeals were not addressed to the proper quarters or —perhaps—were in anticipation of the owners' own researches, which may result in some publications in the near future.

Special thanks and an expression of gratitude are due, on my part, to Professor H. S. Foxwell and Mrs. C. M. Meredith, of Cambridge, who so kindly and disinterestedly assisted me in the rendering of this volume into its English form and the correction of the proofs.

W. R. B.

LONDON, *October*, 1910.

PREFACE TO THE DUTCH EDITION

IT is difficult to review existing conditions in the London Money Market without considering somewhat fully the process of its development. Having become convinced of this during my studies of the theory of banking in England, I changed my original plan, viz., to give a description of the present system of banking, and resolved first of all to devote myself to a description of its historical development. I was strengthened in this resolution by the manner in which the late Dr. N. G. Pierson [1] in the first volume of his *Manual of Political Economy* has dealt with the theory of banking in England.

Some chapters in that work are devoted to the history of the London Money Market, though—as a matter of course—only treated in outline.

In English some four books have appeared dealing with the London Money

[1] Sometime Governor of the Bank of the Netherlands at Amsterdam, and twice Minister of Finance in Holland.

Market. With regard to its history Henry Dunning McLeod's *Theory of Credit* is the most complete, but McLeod does not always show such a desire for truthful elucidation of obscure points by the study of sources as might be expected from a serious historian. J. W. Gilbart's standard work, *Theory and Practice of Banking,* which is considered by practical men to be no longer up to date,[1] does not, as its title shows, deal exclusively with historical development, and whenever Gilbart gives history, it is specially with regard to the Bank of England and the events of the nineteenth century.

With these have to be considered the works of W. Bagehot, *Lombard Street,* and G. Clare, *The London Money Market and Key to the Foreign Exchanges.* Both deal exclusively with the constitution of the London Money Market of the present time, and accept as historical truths what others wrote before them. By this method, however, they failed — in my opinion—to give a complete account. The same may be said of George Rae's *The Country Banker,* a concise manual which is based on practical experience.

Luckily of late some histories of single

[1] A new and revised edition was brought out by Mr. E. Sykes, B.A., Secretary of the Institute of Bankers, in 1907.

banks have appeared which are of great importance in helping to fill the gap. I mean works like Thorold Rogers' *Nine Years of the Bank of England,* F.. G. Hilton Price's *London Bankers,* and Maberly Phillips' *Banks, Bankers, and Banking in Northumberland.* Unfortunately, Thorold Rogers was not able to make use of the records of the Bank of England, which, in my opinion, renders his work incomplete.

Otherwise these books are based on the proper and only reliable sources for an historical study of banking, viz., the still existing records of those institutions.

In Germany, as far as I know, only two descriptions have appeared of the English banking system, viz.: (1) a sketch by Dr. Emil Struck in the *Jahrbücher für Gesetzgebung, Verwaltung,* &c., entitled " Skizze des Englischen Geldmarktes," published in 1887 in pamphlet form ; this describes only the present conditions, though in most attractive form ; and (2) the excellent work of Professor Philippovich von Philippsberg, *Die Bank von England.* This author gives a most careful description of the history of the Bank, though only in its relation to the State.[1]

---

[1] Works like those of Adolph Wagner, Goldsmidt, Tooke, Fullarton, and others chiefly contain theoretical considerations which rest on data collected

Together with these single histories may be mentioned the numerous pamphlets and books which have appeared in England in the nineteenth and former centuries. It had been my intention to add to this book a complete list of the whole of this literature. I was, however, informed that such a bibliography was being prepared by the Bank of England, and would be published very shortly, and I therefore considered it as a needless trespassing on some one else's ground.

I am, therefore, of opinion that this book, though apparently not a finished whole, fills a gap in what has already been published, and—by treating what was left untouched or insufficiently touched—may form a whole with the existing material. There is a second reason which withheld me from extending my description to the fourth and last period of the development of the English Money Market, viz., from 1826 to the present day, the period which is practically of the greatest interest. It was this practical interest which stood in my way. Circumstances prevented me from observing the practice myself.

by others. Wherever they give original research work, this is often of great utility for the proper understanding of the London Money Market, but rather with an eye to present conditions, as they are based on the Act of 1844.

English banks are not accustomed to recruit their staff from any but their own countrymen. And many of the " foreign bankers " seem, unfortunately, not yet to have grasped the idea that scientific investigations may be undertaken without mercenary purposes and may originate in other intentions than those of competition. Information received, as an outsider, from persons who in the busy humdrum of their daily toil take less interest in the " why " and " wherefore " of their actions than in those actions themselves, such information —though always given with the utmost courtesy and kindness—I consider insufficient for the building up of a scientific work, for which one's own observations are absolutely necessary.

In dealing with my subject I have limited the scope of my work to those points which, in my opinion, were of most importance in the development of the English banking *system*. I consider it necessary to point this out in order to avoid the reproach of some hiatus. Two among the subjects which I left untouched call for some notice. Firstly, the important period of the Bank Restriction Act. This period forms a study in itself, but— though it contains a rich mass for investigations regarding the credit system—I am of opinion (and in this I flatter myself that

I share the opinion of one of the most competent authorities on the theory of English banking, Professor Foxwell) that it has contributed very little towards the development of that system. Moreover, I considered its treatment, if so few results were obtainable, too voluminous for this book, and a mere statement of my own opinions regarding this important material would have been needless and out of place.

The second hiatus which I have in view, is the absence of a description of the " bill brokers " and their business. I mentioned the reason in the book itself ; their development took place principally in the fourth period, and for a correct description of their work the history has to be given up to the present day. According to the evidence of Mr. Richardson (at that time the principal " bill broker " in the City) before the Bullion Committee in 1810, these " brokers " were then only bill brokers in the proper sense of the word, intermediaries between the public and the banks. Their business did not begin to develop until after the monopoly of the Bank of England had been repealed, viz., after 1826. They cannot be said to form an essential part of the London Money Market until the second half of the nineteenth century.

The terms " future " and " present

capital " have been taken from Böhm
Bawerk's book *Kapital und Kapitalzins*.
In using them I have tried to follow his
ideas as much as possible, and, if this
assertion be not too bold, to lay a foundation for a future development of the study
of the rate of interest on the London
Money Market along the lines followed
by him.

A few words of thanks to those who
placed me in the position to write what is
contained in the following pages. Especially to the authorities of the Bank of
England, and in particular the late Lord
Aldenham, who were so very kind and
courteous in assisting me to collect data
for the correct interpretation of the ancient
" Goldsmiths' Notes." For similar assistance I must also thank Mr. J. B. Martin,
Director of Martin's Bank, Limited, and
the late Mr. F. G. Hilton Price, partner of
Messrs. Child & Co.

The solution of the real character of
these notes is no matter of indifference,
indeed. If all the ancient documents of
the English financial world from the days
of Cromwell and William III. were public
property, it would not have been necessary
for Professor Goldschmidt in his studies
regarding the laws of bills of exchange and
cheques to content himself with the incomplete data contained in the Venetian

records, and he could have avoided following McLeod—notwithstanding his assertion that this author's historical information has no proper basis—just there his
views rested on hypothesis only.   The
same applies to Dr. Birnbaum, who was
followed by the great scholar.

May benevolence inspire the criticism
of this work !

W. R. B.

THE RISE OF THE LONDON MONEY MARKET

CHAPTER I

1640–1694. THE RISE OF THE LONDON BANKERS

PART I

THE London Money Market is an historical unity which has developed independently of State interference. It is on rare occasions only that we find any interference on the part of the legislature, and even then it is merely to confirm what had previously been accomplished by the merchants or what had gradually become a recognised custom.

In order to understand an organism fully, a thorough knowledge of its historical development is essential. For the purpose of reviewing this history it will not be necessary to go farther back than the sixteenth century. Previously thereto banking in England was completely unknown and the ground entirely unprepared for its advent.

Even as late as the fifteenth century industry in England was not based on capitalistic principles. Wool, the staple product, was exported as it came from the sheep's back, and it was not until some hundreds of years after the import of Flemish weavers into England that cloth became one of the chief articles of export.

Trade was principally carried on by foreign merchants with foreign capital. They had agents established in London and other seaports.

Amongst the articles of import figured coin and bullion ; but the gold and silver which had once entered the country hardly ever left it again, at first on account of the large internal demand for circulating medium, later as a result of the prohibitive measures on " mercantilist " lines. Then the merchants found themselves constrained to confine their exports exclusively to merchandise in other forms.

Payments were effected in hard cash [1] and the exchange of money was forbidden to private persons.[2]

The minting of money was a royal prerogative, but means had not yet been invented to

[1] As far as cash was available. The condition of the Coinage was deplorable. The clipping of money and the importation of base coin was of regular occurrence.

[2] As it was in other countries. Charles I. even established an office for Exchanges.

prevent deterioration in the coinage by constant wear and clipping, so that debasement was often a necessary result of recoinage. Foreign coins had to be exchanged immediately at the "exchange offices" specially designated for this purpose, whence they at once found their way into the crucible in order to be recoined and re-issued in the shape of English shilling pieces.[1]

In addition to this we find the condemnation of usury by public opinion and the canonists and the Legislature, which contemplated the prevention of transactions for the loan of money against interest. In reality, this very opposition led to the exaction of high rates of interest.[2]

Under those conditions the trade in money, pure and simple, could hardly be expected to develop and flourish. Those in need of funds had recourse to borrowing as a last resource only when outstanding debts had to be met or taxes to be paid to the Sovereign. They, of course, looked under such circumstances towards the parties who were best provided

---

[1] Exchange tables had been established at all seaports by command of Edward I. in order to prevent the importation of light coin from abroad.

[2] Cunningham quotes an instance for the fourteenth century when 20 per cent. was paid for three months. In Piacenza the rate of interest was still 40 per cent. in 1490. Business had to be exceedingly remunerative if merchants could afford to pay interest at the rate of 80 per cent. per annum.

3

with cash. As elsewhere, these were either the Jews [1] or foreign merchants.

Long before the expulsion of the Jews [2] the Lombards had settled in London ; they were agents of the Florentine bankers, who had been sent thither in the first instance to collect the Papal taxes.

These taxes probably consisted in the tithes raised by the Church, which were paid in produce and sold in the towns. The funds obtained in this fashion were transmitted to Italy by means of bills of exchange, drawn against shipments of wool. Shipments of actual specie were probably of rare occurrence. In this way the Papal merchants were in a position to accumulate large quantities of silver for which, in view of the fact that wool shipments took place during part of the year only, they naturally endeavoured to find remunerative employment. In order to evade the charge of usury they resorted to various

[1] The constant persecutions to which the Jews were exposed and the numerous prohibitive measures against their acquiring real estate caused them to retain their savings in readily transportable articles of high value. Cunningham goes too far in maintaining that a natural aversion to manual labour, and other less commendable qualities, were the true causes which prompted the Jews to take up the profession of money-lenders.

[2] Properly speaking, this expulsion took place in 1290, in the reign of Edward I., when from 15,000 to 16,000 Jews were compelled to leave the country. A considerable proportion, however, appears either to have stayed or returned, for according to Jewish tradition the year of their expulsion is given as 1358. (See Cunningham, i. p. 267.)

expedients, which, though escaping detection at first, attracted attention ere long.

Soon after the expulsion of the Jews the same complaints were heard about the greed of the foreigners from Italy as formerly of the greed of those from Canaan. The Italians, however, could not be got rid of as easily ; the Florentines were Gentiles and appealed to the Pope. In their case another method was adopted. As early as the reign of Edward I. the monarchs were wont to borrow funds from these merchant money-lenders against a note of hand in their favour. Although powerless to expel their creditors, the Crown could, and in 1339 actually did, ignore its obligations and in this way indirectly compelled them to leave the country.

From agents they had gradually developed into independent merchants. After their departure, their places were filled by others and for long years the street which owes to them its name, "Lombard Street," was the abode of the leading merchants from abroad.[1]

[1] Lombard Street was at one time the market-place, the Exchange. "From what Stone says about Lombard Street, we may judge that the Longobards and other merchants, and strangers of divers nations who were in the habit of frequenting the street twice every day, soon did a large business, and took shops for the purpose. We read that in the twelfth year of Edward II. a certain messuage was set apart for them abutting on Lombard Street on the south and Cornhill on the north, which was the forerunner of the Royal Exchange."
These shops all had signboards, sometimes projecting as

It was only gradually and not until the end of the sixteenth century that they were replaced by the English goldsmiths.

Apart from their current business, the merchants continued to lend money, mostly on security of merchandise.[1]

far as the middle of the street in order to attract as much attention as possible. Originally these signboards presumably indicated at the same time the nature of the "shop," and as the business passed from father to son this presented no obstacle. Later these conditions changed ; Lombard Street became the headquarters of the goldsmiths, but the signboards remained unchanged. They were expressly admitted by Charles I. "for the better finding of the Citizens' dwellings," but prohibited by Charles II. in 1664 on account of the danger which they constituted to pedestrians. They were then first fixed to the buildings, but disappeared with few exceptions between 1762 and 1769.

The best known amongst these signs are, besides "Ye Marygold" of Child & Co., the "Grasshopper" of Martins' Bank, Ltd., the "Black Horse" of Barclay Bevan Tritton & Co. (whose building now also comprises the "Three Kings," "Black Spread Eagle," and the "Ram "), the "Black Bull" of the late Overend Gurney & Co., and also of Glyn Mills Currie & Co. and the "Puntack's Head," formerly Lloyds' Coffee House, now part of the bank of Messrs. Robbarts Lubbock & Co.

As signboards bear an international character they naturally include amongst their number names renowned elsewhere, such as "Adam & Eve," and "The Flying Horse" (Hilton Price, *The Signs of Old Lombard Street*).

[1] Their method of lending money has been preserved, coupled with the name of the Lombards, in the Dutch word *lommerd ;* and the arms of the house of Medici, assumed by the Florentines, viz. three gold balls, still denotes the abode of an ever helpful relative.

The security generally consisted in tangible objects, except where the Government was concerned. But in daily practice it was not likely that this custom was as a hard-and-fast rule strictly adhered to. Cunningham quotes instances where a ersonal guarantee was likewise accepted as security.

The money so employed constituted their own capital, and not the money of others. They were money-lenders, not intermediaries, and could not be considered as bankers.[1]

True, there were brokers, whose occupation consisted in procuring, not always at a modest brokerage, parties willing to lend money. But they remained middlemen ; they never transacted business at their own risk, and it would be equally incorrect to regard them as the precursors of the bankers of a subsequent period.

It was not until the second half of the sixteenth century that England was in a fit state to receive those seeds of banking which have since attained such remarkable development.

The principal preparation consisted in plac-

[1] It was only gradually that this method of granting credit detached itself from general business and began to develop as a separate trade (pawnbroker's).

As regards banking, although the history of banking at Barcelona and the name of the British Linen Company afford evidence that its connection with some branches of trade is not without precedent, yet history demonstrates that in those places where the banking system actually took root it very soon became distinct from other branches of trade, except where special causes prevented such separation. In view thereof it is remarkable, that amongst the 89 guilds of the Corporation of the City of London no bankers' guild exists. The majority of the guilds were instituted about the fourteenth century, when the Florentines were already approaching the end of their golden age.

ing industry on a capitalistic basis. The individual workman recedes into the background and is replaced by the Corporation.[1]

As a result of numerous new discoveries commerce had found fresh outlets and new markets. Many an Englishman was to be found amongst those who ventured across distant seas, and although the new sea-routes and newly-discovered countries were not in the first instance explored with an eye to the establishment of permanent business relations, yet England's trade with the Old World steadily increased, and European countries afforded markets for the produce imported into England from the new regions as well as for English goods. The development of England's industry placed the English more and more in a position to carry on their trade with their own capital. The profits realised by the merchants contributed in no mean degree to the accumulation of this wealth.[2]

In 1546 the prohibition of usury was relaxed

---

[1] *Cf.* Cunningham, p. 466 and following. As an instance the Act of 1555 on the cloth industry may be quoted. In the same year the Mayor and Aldermen of Norwich resolved to import workmen from Naples, at that time the centre of the textile industry, and to provide them with the capital required for their work.

[2] These profits and the consequent increased wealth attracted the attention of their fellow-citizens, who enriched the code of morality with numerous doctrines against covetousness and the love of gain.

and the legal rate of interest fixed at 10 per cent.[1]

Meanwhile the Old World had been inundated—judged by the standards of those days—with precious metals from America, and this country received a liberal share. Nevertheless, the silver coins, the principal national currency, soon became seriously defective both in quantity and in weight. This may be attributed, partly to the way in which wealth in those times was hoarded, viz., in the shape of jewels and precious metals, partly also to the luxurious fashion of the time for plate.[2]

Whilst formerly the metal was actually not available, it now circulated only as light coin, all heavy coin having been withdrawn for hoards or for export.

It will be readily understood that under these circumstances the trade of the goldsmiths became particularly remunerative.[3]

---

[1] The institution of a legal rate of interest did not prevent the goldsmith-bankers of a later period from making 30 per cent. on their money, one of the chief reasons why they were opposed to the establishment of the Bank of England.

[2] Contemporary historians relate how the robes of the ladies of quality were stiff from the gold and jewels with which the silk was literally strewn, not to mention the lace collars and ornamental jewellery. The dress of the gentlemen yielded little in this respect to that of the fair sex. The gold and silver plate and dishes of the classical dynasties seemed to have become reality again in high society at Whitehall.

[3] By *Statute* 28 *Edward I. c.* 20 (1300) it was enacted that the fineness of all gold supplied by any goldsmiths in London

Their guild dates from the end of the thirteenth century, but so far they had not come into greater prominence than any of the other guilds in London. Their trade especially fitted them for the office of inspector of the Mint, and although in this direction no fixed rule was ever observed, we frequently find a goldsmith at the head of the London Mint. Money dealers they were not. Although prohibited by law, the importation and exportation of gold and silver was a common practice, but was confined to the merchants. The fluctuation in the foreign exchanges were a profitable source of income to them, and one which not infrequently gave rise to complaints.[1]

should at least be "of the touch of Paris" whilst a similar provision existed with regard to silver. Of special importance was the condition : "That all the good towns of England where any goldsmiths be dwelling, shall be ordered as they of London be and that one shall come from every good town, for all the residue that be dwelling in the same unto London, for to be ascertained of their touch," which provided for a uniform assay for all cities in England. "This is," adds Cunningham (p. 263), "so far as I know, the earliest instance when the wardens of a Craft Gild were recognised by public authority as the agents through whom a parliamentary enactment should be carried out." And their duties continue thus at the present day.

[1] Cf., i.a., A Treatise of the Canker of England's Commonwealth, by Gerard de Malynes, 1601. The penalties which were threatened against smelting and especially against the clipping of coin were extremely severe. The latter offence was placed on a par with the forging of coin and later with the making of forged banknotes, the penalty for which was capital punishment. The profits must have been huge, if they were worth risking one's life for.

Their practice of buying and selling various kinds of specie from and to merchants and others travelling abroad cannot have been carried on publicly until Elizabeth's reign, since previously thereto the prohibitive measures against the changing of specie in places other than those designated by the King were rigidly enforced. After this time the trade in precious metals assumed a more prominent place amongst their transactions.[1]

The banks and bankers of the European

[1] The metal industry, which presented greater technical difficulties, was gradually pushed into the background. The author of the *Mystery of the Newfashioned Goldsmiths or Bankers* writes : "In my time their whole employment was to make and sell plate, to buy foreign coyns and gold and silver, imported to melt and cull them and cause some to be coyned at the Mint and with the rest to furnish the Refiners, Plate makers and merchants as they found the price of gold and silver to vary and as the merchants had occasion to forreign coyns."

Thirty years later it was, according to Macaulay, customary for them "to traffic largely in the precious metals" ; and once having combined banking with the metal trade, they neglected the industry so completely that at the end of the seventeenth century there were but few traces left in their books which betrayed the origin of the bankers.

Cf. Hilton Price's *Ye Marygold*, p. 17. The ledgers prior to 1690 are much mixed up with banking accounts, goldsmiths' accounts, and occasional pawns' accounts, thus showing that the latter old and profitable branch of a goldsmith's business lingered for a considerable period.

Amongst the Investments and cash of the "Grasshopper," "Pieces of eight" and "French luidores" still figured in 1749, which elicited the following note from Martin, the historian of this house : "A survival of the exchange business carried on by the early Goldsmith."

continent, although known in England, had not, as yet, found imitators in this country.[1]

However, the way was paved for them by the increased spirit of liberty which began to prevail, the efforts made by the Government to foster trade and commerce and the measures which aimed at greater stability in the monetary system.

Amongst the latter we may mention, the closing of all mints in other places than London and the erection of one single mint on Tower Hill for the whole of England. At the commencement of the seventeenth century that single mint was leased to a goldsmith.

A problem which caused much concern to all those possessed of wealth was the selection of a safe place for its custody. At first those buildings were chosen which by their inviolability or their strength were especially adapted to this purpose. Convents were much used. The places where money was coined, and Government institutions which themselves had large quantities of bullion committed to their care, likewise lent themselves to this end, at least in Queen Elizabeth's time. Considerable amounts had thus during the first half of the seventeenth century been entrusted for safekeeping to the London Mint.

[1] The above-mentioned treatise of Malynes, part of which has been reprinted by Cunningham, testifies to this.

Whatever possibilities there might have been that these practices would lead to the foundation of a State Bank were unrealised owing to the untrustworthiness of the Government.

Charles I. closed the Mint in 1640 and appropriated the accumulated fund of the merchants which was stored in its vaults.

These sums were at a later date refunded to the owners, but the Mint had irretrievably lost its reputation for security. Henceforward, the merchants retained their cash themselves, or entrusted one of their clerks, their cashier, with its safe custody. This method was also open to objections. During the Civil War several cashiers proved unable to withstand temptation and deserted to the army of Cromwell—with the funds in their possession. It was then that some merchants commenced to place their cash with goldsmiths so that these latter might receive and effect payments on their behalf. Private persons followed their example. Those who did not consider it safe to retain what they possessed in the shape of precious metals at their own residence deposited it with the goldsmiths for safe-keeping.

These latter were quick to seize the opportunity which thus presented itself. They offered their services as cashiers to all who were willing to deposit their gold and silver

plate, ornaments, metal, or specie with
them.[1]

The goldsmiths made no charge for their
services in this connection, but any deposit
made in any other shape than ornaments was
looked upon by them as a free loan. The
cash left in their hands remained " at call."

In order to extend their business in this
direction they induced the cashiers who had
remained faithful to deposit their masters'
cash with them in consideration of an allow-
ance of 4d. per cent. interest per day.[2]

Almost simultaneously the deposit and
current account system had come into use.

---

[1] "Before the end of the reign of Charles II. a new mode
of paying and receiving money had come into fashion
among the merchants of the capital. A class of agents arose,
whose office was to keep the cash of the commercial houses. . .
When in 1680, after residing many years abroad he [Sir Dudley
North] returned to London, nothing astonished or displeased
him more than the practice of making payments by drawing
bills on bankers. He found that he could not go on 'Change
without being followed round the piazza by goldsmiths, who,
with low bows, begged the honour of serving him " (Macaulay,
Chap. XX).

Those who enjoyed most confidence were, *i.a.*, entrusted
with the collection of the rents on behalf of the landlords when
the latter had returned to town.

[2] About 6 per cent. per annum. As a result of the fact that
interest was allowed on deposits and that the big landlords
spent a considerable part of the year in London a flow of
money from all parts of the country converged upon the
metropolis. Josiah Child in his *New Discourse of Trade*
justly complains of this, "for the trade of bankers being only
in London, doth very much drain the ready money from all
other parts of the Kingdom."

From this time it continued to form the principal part of their business, and this was indicated by the description given of them, viz., " Goldsmiths—that keep running cashes."

They did not allow these funds to lie idle. Very soon a business in precious metals was carried on by them on a scale which far surpassed anything hitherto achieved in this way by the merchants.[1]

They had promptly learned to appreciate the fact that the moneys entrusted to their care, although they were deposited at call, would not all be withdrawn simultaneously, and that fresh deposits would continue to replace those which were recalled. Relying on this " running cash," they began to lend out funds, at first for weeks, then for months, to discount bills (to supply merchants with hard cash for their bills of exchange) at a rate of discount varying " as they found the merchants more or less pinched." They

[1] About the time of Cromwell's dictatorship new half-crowns were minted to the amount of £7,000,000. As a result of the primitive methods employed the coins were not all of uniform weight and sometimes even differed to the extent of from 2d. to 3d. per ounce. The goldsmiths who handled them in large quantities had little difficulty in weighing and melting down the heaviest pieces. The silver thus melted down was exported to France in such quantities that after a very short time the amount in circulation had been reduced to £1,000,000 and the public continued to complain of the excessive number of light and clipped coins (cf. Mystery of the Newfashioned Goldsmiths).

also lent to private persons " to dispose of money for more than lawful interest, either upon Pawns or Bottom,[1] reason- or unreasonable discounts of Interests for Bills, or upon notorious usurious Contracts, or upon personal Securities from Heirs whose Estates are in expectancy, or by sudden advance of money to Projectors, who drawn into Projects many Responsible men to the ruin of their Families." [2] And after Cromwell had assumed the reins of Government, the chief amongst them opened negotiations with him and provided him with money in return for very liberal remuneration. This example was followed by others. When the monarchy had been reinstated Charles II. found not one, but several, bankers prepared to advance him money against Treasury Notes, secured on the taxes.[3]

The goldsmiths provided the funds which were required as soon as Parliament had sanctioned the raising of fresh taxes, whilst re-

[1] Bottomry, which even in the eighteenth century formed a favourite manner of granting advances. A variant thereof were the so-called " Respondentia Bonds " of which the Cargo constituted the security (cf. Martin's Grasshopper, p. 156).

[2] Cf. Mystery of the Newfashioned Goldsmiths. Evidently a goldsmith was not a persona grata in everybody's eyes.

[3] "These Bankers undertook to lend him not their own, but other men's money, taking barefaced of Him ten pound for the hundred, and by private contracts many Bills, Orders, Tallies and Debts of the King's, above twenty, and sometimes thirty in the hundred, to the great dishonour of the Government" (cf. Mystery of the Newfashioned Goldsmiths).

payments were effected in weekly instalments varying in amount according to the incoming receipts from these taxes.   Generally these transactions extended over three or four years : for the goldsmiths they constituted an important source of income, and to many of them these loans soon became the principal field for the employment of their capital.   The Exchequer [1] was generally well provided with money when Parliament was favourably disposed towards the Government.

Again, however, temptation proved too strong for the Government, and in January, 1672, the goldsmiths received notification that

[1] The Exchequer had been founded by William the Conqueror, and was consequently one of the oldest public institutions in England.   The King's accounts were kept, taxes collected and all payments effected by this Court (which accompanied the King to the various places where he held residence).   At the same time one of the functions assigned to the Exchequer was the trial of all disputes arising out of the collection of taxes. Afterwards these two functions were separated and entrusted to two distinct bodies.   Upon the Exchequer Court the duty of administering justice in general was conferred and it became a Supreme Court ; the Exchequer Treasury confined itself to public functions, whilst the Administration of the King's private financial affairs was assigned to the Treasury, which was attached to the former.

Treasury and Exchequer are at present practically merged again.

The name is derived from the French *échecs, exchiquier,* chessboard, though Blackstone states that the Court was called the Exchequer from the chequered cloth which covered the table.   Chessboards were frequently used in calculations relating to money.   Each square represented a certain figure. Hence the expression " to check an account."

the funds deposited by them in the Treasury had been confiscated, and that repayment of the moneys advanced by them to the Exchequer would be discontinued. This time the sums so confiscated were never refunded.[1]

This was a national calamity, the more so

[1] The debt was subsequently acknowledged to the extent of one half, say £664,262, and still constitutes the first item of the English National Debt. It was afterwards consolidated with the South Sea Annuities.

Charles I. promised to pay 6 per cent. on the capital out of his private purse. His intention was communicated by letters, couched in identical terms, to all concerned. The way in which the King expressed his regret for what had occurred seems sufficiently remarkable for reproduction : " Charles the Second, by the grace of God, of England, Scotland, France and Ireland King, Defender of the Faith etc. To all to whom these presents shall come Greeting, Whereas since the time of our happy Restoration We have been involved in great Forreigne Warrs as well for the Safety of our Government as the vindication of the Rights and Privileges of our Subjects, In the prosecution whereof we have been constreyned for some years past, contrary to our Inclinacions, to postpone the payment of the moneys due from Us to several Goldsmiths and other upon Tallys struck and Orders Registered on and payable out of severall Branches of Our Revenue and otherwise, And although the present Posture of Our affaires cannot reasonably spare so greate a sum as must be applyed to the satisfaction of those debts, Yet considering the great difficulty which very many of our Loving Subjects (who putt their moneys into the hands of those Goldsmiths and others from whom we received it) doe at present Lye under, almost to their utter ruine for want of their said moneys, We have rather chose out of our princely care and compassion towards Our people, to suffer in Our owne Affaires than that our loving subjects should want soe reasonable a Reliefe.' "

This was to consist in the payment at 6 per cent. to the victims and their heirs—a promise, however, which was only kept for the period 1677–83.

as during the period of thirty-two years, thus concluded, the custom of depositing money with the modern bankers had become so universal that, when several goldsmiths were compelled to suspend payment, not only merchants but widows and orphans were found to be amongst the victims.

By this action the Crown had completely forfeited public confidence, and was obliged to provide for its financial requirements in other ways. Meanwhile its resources were limited to the proceeds of the taxes, which came in very irregularly. The taxes began to be oppressive. Means had to be devised to restore confidence in the Crown, without imposing too heavy a burden on the public. Shortly after the Revolution a solution was found : posterity, the taxpayers of the future, were saddled with the obligations which would otherwise have devolved upon the living generation. The system of funded debt was established under William III. Thus he was able to borrow large sums without proportionately increasing the burden of taxation, and those who supplied him with capital were protected against loss ; they were aware that the sums lent would never be repaid, but that the regular annual payment of interest was assured. For the due performance thereof the proceeds of the taxes constituted a security.

Meanwhile the goldsmiths continued to

carry on their banking business.   Not all had
been hit by the calamity of 1672,[1] and those
who previous to that year had remained in
the background, took advantage of the gaps
which had thus been created in their ranks.[2]

PART II

THIS marked the close of the first period of
the development of the London Money Market,
during which evolution proceeded without
any encouragement on the part of the
Government.

Before its history is further pursued, a few
explanatory remarks may be allowed on the
system so far built up.

[1] Charles Duncombe (goldsmith at the "Grasshopper") was
among the more fortunate ones.   "No doubt with a keen eye
to his own interests, as well as to the welfare of his banker,
Shaftesbury conveyed to him a timely warning of the imminent
closing of the Exchequer and by this means he was enabled to
withdraw very great sums of his own and £30,000 belonging to
the Marquis of Winchester, afterwards Duke of Bolton.   This
latter action stood him in good stead later on" (cf. The
Grasshopper).

[2] The fact that during the years of war and internal disturbance no goldsmith suspended payment affords evidence of the
sound basis on which the credit of these bankers was by
that time established.

Pepys "did mightily wonder at the growth of the credit of
bankers (since it is so ordinary a thing for citizens to break out
of knavery).   Upon this we had much discourse, and I observed
thereon, to the honour of this City, that I have not heard of one
citizen of London broke in all this war, this plague, or this fire,
and the coming up of the enemy among us" (Pepys' Diary,
September 27, 1667).

It was not until the goldsmiths had become intermediaries, until they received funds from others and supplied them to third parties on loan, that banking can be said to have been exercised in London as a separate profession

It will be convenient to treat each side of their business separately.

On the one hand the banker receives money, coin and bullion. For the sake of brevity, these will be designated by the name of " present capital." [1]

In exchange the banker gives a receipt, an acknowledgment of debt, a promise to pay : in other words, a right to demand capital

---

[1] We admit that this definition implies a considerable restriction of the notion generally entertained of "present capital," viz., the capital which is available in tangible and finished form, but as "present capital" is never transferred to a bank in any other form but gold and silver coin and bullion, the use of the term in this connection will not be likely to cause confusion.

Under "future capital" we do not class the unfinished product, but only those rights which, in political economy, are not set down as capital. A bank never receives either unfinished or finished products, but always the mere right to dispose of such a product at some time or other. Such product, though it may long since have existed in a finished condition, always forms part of the capital which is in existence at that given time. A promise to pay, a bill of exchange, constitutes a right to receive capital which will have to be satisfied at some future date out of the amount of " present capital" then available. To that extent it bears a future character. For the sake of brevity and convenience such documents will be designated by the name of "future capital," in order to avoid the term "credit" which is capable of being interpreted in such a variety of ways. It is not intend however to regard credit as a subdivision of capital.

which either is already in existence, but cannot be disposed of, or which will not be available until some future time. The latter will be called " future capital "—that is to say, capital of which the holder of such an acknowledgment of debt cannot take possession until some future date, even though this date may not be more remote than one single day, and though he may at any moment be able to dispose of it.

The owner of future capital may, by exchange, become possessor of about an equal quantity of present capital ; but as long as he does not avail himself of this opportunity, he is debarred from the use of the latter.[1]

On the other hand, the banker receives " future capital " in the shape of a bill of exchange, or an acknowledgment of debt, and gives in exchange " present capital," or coin or bullion.

At the time of the goldsmith-bankers the elements of all forms of the trade, of all the branches into which it is now subdivided and which only gradually attained their full development, were already in existence. The simple method of transfer above referred to

---

[1] To use a comparison : A person owns a well ; he has the opportunity at all times to draw water from this well, but he cannot use this water for quenching his thirst until he has availed himself of the opportunity. There is many a slip between the cup and the lip.

was most frequently used. The fact is evidenced by their books.

Whether the so-called " Goldsmiths' Notes " could be compared with banknotes has long remained an open question. Thus put, it is a difficult one to solve, for it cannot be stated with precision what the term " Goldsmiths' Note " implies. The precursors of the London bankers issued two kinds of notes. It is probable that both kinds are comprised under one generic name. Under this name should be classed in the first place " the Running Cash Notes."

In form these notes bore the character of receipts.[1]

Those who had deposited their gold and silver plate with the goldsmiths for safe-keeping received a list specifying every article so deposited and containing a classification of the coins. These lists were *deposit receipts* pure and simple, issued against deposits

---

[1] The distinction made by Macleod in his *History and Practice of Banking*, vol. i., p. 282, is devoid of all foundation. It is a conjecture which was accepted as correct by Birnbaum (*Zeitschrift f. d. Ges. Handelsrecht*, No. 30, p. 3), and taken over from him by Goldschmidt (*Universal Geschichte des Handelsrechts*, p. 327). According to his assertions there were Bankers' Notes and Cash Notes. The latter were supposed to be equal to cheques ; Macleod quotes their text as it is still preserved at Child's Bank, "Pray pay," &c. "Cash Notes," as he understood them, were drawn by the depositor himself, and not by the banker. Against this supposition the Minute Books of the Bank of England afford incontrovertible evidence (*cf.* pp. 106 *et seq.*).

effected for purposes of safe-keeping. When the deposits became deposits of money (cash), the form of the receipt was retained for the total amount. Whenever a payment was made, the amount by which the debt had been reduced was written off on this document, whilst interest was allowed on the amounts left in the hands of the banker during a certain period.

The notes were probably issued for odd sums.[1]

It is practically certain that notes for round sums were in circulation ; no doubt this chiefly depended upon the magnitude of the deposits against which they were issued. Their circulation was confined to a limited circle.

The following method of transfer of capital found wider application.

At first depositors were obliged to exhibit the list of their deposits each time when they desired to withdraw a portion thereof, or to

---

[1] From the books of Child & Backwell which have been preserved, this cannot be ascertained with certainty. They merely contain a record that certain sums have been paid out and received in notes. These sums are odd amounts. As regards the number in circulation, this can hardly have been very important. The notes issued generally returned from circulation within a week. If a certain number of notes were handed in *en bloc* to a banker by whom they had not been issued originally, the depositor frequently received from the banker to whom they had been transferred a promissory note for their total amount. These Promissory Notes likewise were for odd amounts. As a rule the notes were issued in favour of fellow-goldsmiths.

transfer it to third parties. This necessitated their personal attendance on such occasions. For convenience sake that personal attendance was gradually done away with. A document in writing was addressed to the goldsmith, requesting him to hand to the bearer of the list, whose name was mentioned, the articles of which delivery was desired. Again, the presentation of the list on every occasion when payment was demanded, was also open to objection, the more so since the deposits had lost their original character of " deposits for safe custody." When, finally, this latter requirement was dropped, the ordinary cheque had come into being.[1]

The list is replaced by a book in which the account current of the customer with his banker is kept—that is to say, a copy of the account current in the books of the goldsmith.

[1] As an instance we reproduce a request of this nature addressed to Messrs. Child & Co., Ye Marygold, Strand :

"Bolton, 4th March, 1684.

"At sight hereof pray pay unto Charles Duncombe, Esq., or order, the Sum of four hundred pounds, and place it to the account of

"Your assured friend
"Winchester."

Duncombe at that time was a goldsmith at the "Grasshopper," Lombard Street. This is by no means one of the earliest documents in the shape of a cheque. Amongst the relics of the "Grasshopper" a letter is still in existence, dated 12th April, 1671, by which the same Duncombe requests his clerk Backwell to "pay to Phil Marsh or bearer" the sum of £489.

Similar books are still in use at the present day in the shape of " Pass Books." [1]

Second amongst the goldsmiths' notes rank their " promissory notes." It seems very probable that the latter were the precursors of the banknote of a subsequent period. Pepys' entry in his diary on February 29, 1667-8 is one of the earliest records in which

[1] I am somewhat more positive on this subject than Martin, who is not certain whether the Bank of England in 1694 created the custom of keeping pass books or whether it adopted these from the goldsmiths. At the first Board meeting in that year of the Directors of the Bank of England it was resolved "after debate, that copies of customers' accounts should be kept either in books or on paper of their own." In my opinion the emphasis should be laid on the last three words. It seems improbable that a new body governed by city men, who were not banking experts, should have introduced an entirely new method of administration, whilst the practice of issuing lists of the articles and specie deposited had been in existence for such a long time prior to 1694.

The oldest pass book of private bankers of which anything definite is known dates back to 1709. In *Ye Marygold* Mr. Price narrates that in 1715 Lady Carteret requested Messrs. Child & Co. to send her " a book as I used to have at Mr. Mead's with an account of all you have received." In 1713 a similar request had been addressed to them.

It was customary for those keeping an account-current to verify each year towards Christmas their account in the ledger and to countersign the same with their initials or with the words "allowed by me." Mr. Price found that this custom was already in vogue in 1663.

At the same time the customer handed to the clerk a gratuity. These gratuities were known as " perquisites." This custom was maintained in some old-fashioned banks until quite recently. When for various reasons Martin's Bank put a stop to this practice the amount of this annual liberality was found to be from £1,000 to £1,200.

reference is made to such promissory notes :
" Wrote to my father and sent him Colvil's
note for £600 for my sister's portion."
Among the Promissory Notes of Messrs. Child
& Co. which are still in existence, is one
of the year 1684, which runs as follows :

Nov. 28, 1684.

" I promise to pay unto the Rt. Honble.
Ye Lord North and Grey or bearer,
ninety pounds at demand.
For Mr. Francis Child and myself
Jno. Rogers."

The oldest note of the Bank of England
which has been preserved also contains the
words :

" I promise to pay *Mr. John Wright* or
Bearer on Demand the summe of
two hundred Pounds.

London the *23* day of *Jan. 1699*
200 pd. st.   For the Govr. and Compy.
of the Bank of England
Joseph

It is conceivable that as a promise to
pay, the promissory note bore a character
different from the Running Cash Note. This
view is supported by the history of the promissory note.[1]

---

[1] *Cf. History of the Bank of England,* a small book published
in 1797.

The promissory note is of a very ancient date. It was one of the forms of a " bill of debt." Judge Doddridge in his little work, *The Touchstone of Public Assurance*, 1641, mentioned some twelve or thirteen forms of bills, *inter alia* " Memorandum, I owe and promise to pay."

These "bills of debt " were also known as " bills obligatory."

Prior to 1590 these bills were personal and not transferable. From that year it was permissible to transfer them by endorsement, at first exclusively to persons who were expressly mentioned on the instrument ; subsequently, when this condition was no longer obligatory and notes were made out " to order," to others as well.

It was not until much later, however, that this concession was made. The *Lex Mercatoria* of 1622 draws attention to the banking paper in circulation in Amsterdam, Middelburg, and Hamburg, and to the great advantage to be derived from the readily transferable nature of such documents.

In 1651 a public notary, named John Manus, also draws attention to the desirability of this system, and urges English merchants to follow the example. Either at the time of the Commonwealth or shortly afterwards, the more convenient mode of transfer to order was generally adopted.

The popularity enjoyed by this form of document is chiefly due to the goldsmiths, who availed themselves freely of it. Their promissory notes were similar to the earlier " bills of debt," with the peculiarity, copied from the Continent, that they were not " sealed," but merely signed. Yet it would seem unlikely that these notes were at the time anything beyond ordinary deposit receipts or promissory notes issued to depositors of specie in order to facilitate the transfer of funds and the making of payments.

From the books of the goldsmith-bankers it does not appear whether they were issued in exchange for future capital. The pamphlets of their contemporaries afford no evidence that notes were ever issued against anything but cash.[1] Yet the issue of banknotes by the

---

[1] Thus Francis Craddocke in his *Wealth Discovered* (1661), p. 5 : "So that I hope there is no ingenuous reader but will allow that payments are and may be made upon the credit of money, as well as by money in specie, by transferring the Ownership thereof either by Bill or in Bank, from one person to another, both which are of daily practice in the Low Countries and other parts abroad, and found to be of great advantage in Trade, the first of Bills being much used in England, under the name of Bills of Exchange, though in as improper a method (for want of Lawes suitable to those of Holland) as the shops of Lombard Street (which are banks in effect) may be esteemed, when compared with the richest and best governed Banks of other Nations."

The term "transferring . . . in Bank" is explained as meaning "the transfer of a balance in the books of the Bank."

Craddocke then proceeds to inquire why, if such "credit of money" could be given against a deposit of money, it should

Bank of England was afterwards characterised as a new departure !

The notes of the goldsmiths were—such is the supposition—entirely based upon the objects deposited with them. The entire absence at the present day of any specimens of a Running Cash Note, although these notes are frequently referred to in the books of the goldsmiths, and the fact that of the promissory notes several specimens are still in existence— in connection with what has already been re-marked on the subject, the short currency of the notes, the gradual adoption of cheques as an instrument of payment and the evidence afforded by the books of the Bank of England —all this would lead to the conclusion that the Running Cash Notes were merely receipts which were cancelled as soon as the deposit had been paid in its entirety, and that they were issued for odd sums. They should be considered as the earliest examples of the

not likewise be feasible on the security of goods, jewels, and other pledges, as practised in other countries.

This pamphlet is of an earlier date than any goldsmiths' note within our knowledge. Craddocke is one of the first who considers the establishment of a bank desirable, on the basis outlined by him. He is by no means the last.

Successive authors give expression to the same desire. The idea became gradually better worked out and assumed a more practical form, yet intrinsically it remained the same. This affords evidence of the fact that there was a want left unprovided for, as well in substance as in detail.

More detailed reference to this matter will be found in Chapter II. Part II.

deposit receipts which are still in use at the present day.

The promissory note, on the other hand, was a promise to pay to the depositor, order or bearer, a certain sum out of the funds which he deposited with the banker, and the sum for which it was issued would, as a rule, be in relation to the payments which he had to make. This form was probably selected because it made the note easily transferable, and it was perhaps to facilitate such transfers that the notes were issued for round sums.[1]

Notwithstanding the variety of ways in which customers could dispose of their capital, the basis remained unaltered, viz., the goldsmiths received present capital from their

[1] Martin's Bank, Ltd., still have in their possession a "notebook" containing the amounts which the firm owed to various persons in respect of their deposits. In a balance-sheet, dated Christmas, 1746, and reproduced in the *Grasshopper* (pp. 134, 135), the amount owing to each customer is mentioned in the final column, whilst the adjoining column contains particulars of the debt, viz., whether it represents the balance of a sum previously deposited or whether it is in the shape of a "promissory note." It is conceivable that in former times the amount of such balance was represented by a Running Cash Note on which, of course, no record appeared of the amount repaid.

Due to Sundrys in the Note-Book at Christmas 1746.

Folio to						£	sh.	d.
I. Richard Harris	Dato 27 July 1737	remd	70	0	0	19	10	0
II. David Clayton	I Nov. 1746		100	0	0			
			50	0	0			
			50	0	0	225	0	0
			25	0	0			
15. David Clayton	8 do		350			150	0	0

clients in exchange for future capital, and *vice versâ*. In these transactions the goldsmiths were limited to the amount of present capital which had been transferred to them. As long as these conditions existed, and nothing took place beyond an exchange of two quantities which were dissimilar in character, the goldsmiths' shops remained depositories of present capital, which, at the same time, continued to form the sole basis of their credit system.

Towards the end of the seventeenth century this was the position held by the goldsmiths.[1]

It is true that another mode of granting credit was known to these private bankers,[2]

---

[1] In the Bank Charter Act of 1694 we find that the Bank of England is authorised "to borrow or give security by bills or agreement, under their common seal, for any sum or sums of money," provided the original capital of £1,200,000 is not exceeded ; in other words, provided they do not lend out more money than has actually been entrusted to them.

[2] Amongst others we find in the spring of 1663 an item in Alderman Backwell's books, recording a deposit made by Queen Charlotte (probably the wife of Charles I.), of a tally for £2,000 payable in September ; that is to say, she gave future capital—a claim on the Crown—and received future capital, viz., the right to dispose at any time of this sum. Of this right she actually availed herself on four different occasions by means of cheques. The Government generally borrowed against personal security. They issued "tallies," pieces of wood divided into two symmetrical halves, which were readily accepted and remained in circulation. Against these the goldsmiths frequently gave notes and book credits. The bulk, however, must have been paid over in specie, otherwise Charles II. could not have derived much advantage from the closure of the Exchequer.

at least to those of the goldsmiths who were established in the City, and who were as a rule a few years ahead of their colleagues in the West End. However, with the sole exception of the Crown, the method outlined above was the one usually followed.

The main point to a banker is, no doubt, that the depositor should withdraw as little as possible of the capital entrusted to his bank ; and, if he does withdraw, that the sums in question should flow back to the bank with as little delay as possible, so that the banker may always be in a position to lend all present capital received by him to third parties.

This he may do in either of two ways.

He may promote the circulation of the promissory notes which are issued by him. The holder of such notes is owner of future capital, and the person who is prepared to take over these notes gives present capital in exchange. This can be carried through if the banker or the bank is widely known and enjoys public confidence, but even then only over a limited area. Several years elapsed before the Bank of England succeeded in having its notes freely accepted.

Future capital may also remain in circulation in the shape of book credits. In such case, the right to dispose of the capital goes from hand to hand, but is restricted to those parties who have the same banker. In order to carry this through the banker requires an extensive *clientèle*, a monopoly or a close understanding between himself and his various colleagues.

It requires a greater exertion in labour and time to create an extensive *clientèle* than to become widely known and to command public confidence.

If we take this circumstance into account, and also the fact that the deposit receipts were the forerunners of the banknotes, it will be understood why in the eighteenth century " banking " was considered to consist chiefly of receiving deposits and issuing banknotes. Much later, after closer relations had been established between the London banks, the cheque system began to develop.

It has already been pointed out that the goldsmith-bankers derived the greater part of their profit from operating with the funds entrusted to them. Apart from their business as money dealers, they granted advances on security at high rates of interest. In such case they received future capital and gave present in return.

The large profits were due to the high premiums which present capital commanded, especially in those days when it was scarce.

The Jews and Florentines had already taken advantage of this and realised huge profits, but they had employed their own capital. The goldsmiths of the seventeenth century lent capital which they had received from others.[1]

This had been done long before their time, by the Italian bankers. When, with increasing certainty of legal protection and hence greater likelihood that the capital lent will be repaid—in other words, that the future capital will one day actually be present capital—bankers learn by experience that the funds deposited with them are generally not withdrawn in their entirety, but that a certain proportion is permanently left in their hands, they begin to look for means of employing this permanent portion more remuneratively.

As the waves appear on the surface of the sea only whilst the deep water remains undisturbed, subject merely to the regular current and tides, so the bulk of the banking deposits

[1] As soon as the surplus funds, instead of being hoarded in the vaults of the Mint, were deposited with bankers, in exchange for future capital, the said bankers were in a position to exercise also the second, that is to say the active, part of the banking business.

By granting advances on security they practically continued the business of the pawnbrokers of former centuries. Afterwards this business remained in the hands of the goldsmiths. Those who did not adapt themselves to banking, and continued their old industry, often retained this source of income. Even at the present day, though it may not be a universal practice, one frequently finds the business of pawnbroker combined with that of "silversmith, goldsmith, and jeweller." It is a retrograde step, for the parties in question have reverted to the method of supplying money out of their own capital.

remain invariably at the bank. The owners of the future capital issued against it may change names and succeed each other in regular rotation, as do the drops of water in the Gulf Stream—the fluctuations of the moment are not perceptible therein. They remain within the limits of a maximum and a minimum.

The more business expands the greater the need of present capital.

Present capital can only be supplied after the deposit has acquired the character of a loan, instead of being merely money left in safe keeping—that is to say, after the bankers have obtained full ownership of the present capital for which they gave future capital in return.

The right to procure capital in this way was not recognised for a long time. Nay, the right to use at discretion the capital thus secured has been the subject of constant interference on the part of the legislator, in so far, at least, as the banks played a part in the monetary system of the country. In Venice the recognition of this right was only obtained after a prolonged struggle. In England the principle of individual liberty has always prevented any legal restrictions from being imposed upon the goldsmiths, or at a later period upon the Bank of England.

But the nature of the business itself provided a restriction. Bankers are always obliged to advance less than has been entrusted to them. A portion has to be retained as a reserve, for emergencies, in case the minimum of deposits should sink below the usual level.

Generally speaking, the period required to transform the future capital, entrusted to the bankers, into present capital should be longer than the loans supplied by them to others.

This rule has not always been observed, either in England or in other countries, and its neglect has frequently entailed serious consequences.

Besides making advances on security, the goldsmiths discounted bills and supplied the Government with funds. The former operation did not come into prominence until much later, whilst the latter constituted a purely private transaction. The King offered himself as surety ; and although the proceeds of the taxes were assigned as security for the repayment of the loans, the collection of these taxes in England was not leased to the contractors of the loan as was customary in other European countries. Hence the serious shock when the King appeared to be untrustworthy, and all security was absolutely useless to the goldsmiths, as it was impossible to make use of it.

CHAPTER II

1694–1742. THE DEVELOPMENT OF THE MONO-POLY OF THE BANK OF ENGLAND

PART I

ONCE the idea of entering into perpetual loan operations with the Government had become popular there was no lack of proposals to put it into execution. Soon after William III. had ascended the throne, bills were laid before the House of Commons, to provide for the payment of annuities in return for the advance of a capital sum. Those who had suffered in 1672 owing to the closure of the Exchequer, were allowed 3 per cent. annuities, charged on the hereditary excise, which were counted as redemption of their capital.[1]

Twice William Paterson submitted a proposal which was to provide the King with the

---

[1] This at a time when pamphlets on the appropriateness of the creation of a bank on the same basis as that of the banks abroad were prolific. William Potter (in 1650) and Craddocke (in 1660) had already drawn attention to the advantage which might be derived by the Government from such an institution.

necessary funds, whilst those who advanced
the money were to be considered as founders
of a National Bank. Each time his efforts
were in vain.

In 1694 Michael Godfrey and some others
who experienced financial difficulties in connection with the East India Company, invoked
Paterson's aid. A third project was devised
on the same lines as the two former ones.
In consideration of an annual payment of
£100,000 the promoters undertook to find
a capital of £1,200,000 on behalf of the
Government. Thanks to their influence, this
scheme was successful.

On April 25, 1694, the Bank Charter Act [1]
received the Royal sanction. On June 15th the
charter was signed, and within ten days the
entire amount of £1,200,000 had been subscribed. On July 27th the Deed of Incorporation was executed and on the same date the
Governor and Company of the Bank of
England commenced operations in Mercers'
Chapel.[2]

The wish had frequently been expressed
that the State should derive advantage from
the trade established by the Goldsmiths, or, in
other words, that a State Bank should be
founded.

Those responsible for the formation of the
Bank of England had this time forestalled

[1] 5 and 6 W. nd M. c. 20.
[2] On June 1, 1695, the Bank removed to Grocers' **Hall.**

the Government. The main object was that the King should be provided with the where-withal to carry on the war with France. The Government undertook to pay annually by way of interest a sum representing 8 per cent. of the principal.[1] This interest had to be found from the proceeds of certain new taxes. For the imposition of fresh taxes for special purposes Parliamentary sanction was required. Hence the Bank Charter Act provides in the first place for the raising of tonnage dues on vessels, for an excise on beer, wine, and other alcoholic beverages, and secondly stipulates that out of the proceeds of such taxes £140,000 shall be set aside annually and handed over to those who will advance to the Government the sum of £1,500,000 for a period of at least eleven years.

In order to insure the success of the issue the subscription list remained open for three months. In addition a privilege was granted to the subscribers, viz., that they, as a body, were to constitute a company, which would have the right to carry on banking business— *i.e.*, to receive money on deposit, to deal in bills of exchange, in gold and silver ; to grant advances on security of merchandise with the right to realise that security in case the advances were not repaid and to reim-

---

[1] Eight per cent. was the usual rate paid by the Government. The Goldsmiths allowed 6 per cent. on their deposits.

burse themselves out of the proceeds ; to issue promissory notes transferable by endorsement.

This explains why the basis of an institution which was soon to exercise so considerable an influence on England's finances, and was to form with them a united system, was contained in an ordinary bill of supply and, in that, in scattered and loosely connected clauses only.[1]

To the Government it was of the highest importance to find funds for the war against France. A great number of provisions had been included in the bill as to the manner of subscribing, the sums for which each sub-scriber might participate, the time during which the subscription lists should remain open to the public, provisions in case of failure, and regarding the deposit of the funds sub-scribed for with the Treasury. Interest at 10 per cent. until September, 1694, was offered for payments made before that date. In order to enlist the support of Parliament, it was provided that members of that assembly should be admitted as subscribers. It was expressly added in the final paragraphs that if in this way the necessary funds should not

[1] Much against the wish of the Lords, who considered their rejection on the ground that such clauses were not essential to a money bill, afraid as they were that the establishment of the Bank would deter the public from investing in land and reduce its saleableness. (Cf. Secret Correspondence of N. de l'Hermitage with the States General of the Netherlands, No. 124, dated April 30, 1694, British Museum, MS.)

b'e forthcoming the Government would be authorised to provide for its financial requirements by the issue of a loan.

The main question was whether Parliament would be disposed to grant the King fresh taxes. This point formed the nucleus of the deliberations, and on that issue the final division was taken.[1]

In the House no marked opposition was shown against the establishment of a bank in itself. It was against the granting of a privilege to City merchants and the abandonment by the Government of profits which they might have reaped themselves that criticism was chiefly directed.[2] Another objection was not entirely devoid of foundation, viz., that the Government might thus be enabled to raise money at any time through the Bank without the knowledge of Parliament.

To prevent this, Clause 30 was inserted, expressly prohibiting the Bank Directors, on penalty of a fine, to make advances to the Government on the revenue unless parliamentary sanction had previously been given.

The Act of 1694 was an act of ways and

[1] For particulars regarding these deliberations and the history of the passing of the Act, *cf.* Chap. XX. of Macaulay's *History.*

[2] The fact that the opposition in Parliament to the Bill which was afterwards Act 5 and 6 William and Mary, c. 20, was of a purely political character, is proved by the composition of the group who opposed the scheme, and which consisted of the Tory members and the Dissentient Whigs.

means, a taxation act, in which special provisions had been inserted in favour of those
who supplied the Government with the funds
of which it so sorely stood in need.

The strongest antagonism against the establishment of a bank naturally emanated from
the goldsmith-bankers, who realised that the
competition of an institution founded under
Government auspices was likely to be prejudicial to their interests.[1] This hostile attitude
was persisted in during the first years of the
Bank's existence and frequent endeavours
were made to compel the Bank to suspend
payment.[2]

They were supported in this attitude by
the projectors of rival schemes, to which
reference will be made later.

In spite of all this the establishment of
the Bank was carried out. Its capital was to
be in stock. It was not divided into shares of
a fixed denomination.

Every subscriber became a shareholder for
the amount of his participation, which could
not exceed £10,000. Any part thereof could
be transferred to others. The amount thus

[1] Especially as the Bank was entitled to grant interest on
deposits at the rate of 3 per cent. p.a. The Goldsmiths did not
pay any interest on deposits. (*Cf.* de l'Hermitage, *Secret
Correspondence*, No. 123, April 27, 1694, and No. 127, May 25,
1694.)

[2] See on this point Cunningham, chap. ii. ; Thorold Rogers,
The First Nine Years of the Bank of England, and Macleod,
Theory of Credit, vol. i.

raised—viz., £1,200,000 [1]—constituted the original capital of the Bank of England and at the same time the limit of its banking operations.

The condition of the coinage in those days, as was so frequently the case, both at previous and subsequent periods, left much to be desired.[2] Clipped coins were nearly exclusively met with in circulation ; the unclipped and heavy coins were exported in large quantities. Several measures were taken by the Government to stop this evil, though in the beginning the means adopted were not always the most appropriate.[3]

On January 21, 1696, the Recoinage Act was placed on the Statute Book. New coins were minted (this time " milled " coins) and it was provided that the old light coins should not be tolerated in circulation beyond February 1, 1697.

If, however, circulating medium is withdrawn in one form, unless it is replaced in another, shortage will ensue.

---

[1] According to par. 19 of the Act, those who subscribed "for and towards the raising and paying into the receipt of the Exchequer the said sum of twelve hundred thousand pounds part of the sum of fifteen hundred thousand pounds " were to constitute jointly "the Company of the Bank of England." The interest was guaranteed by setting aside £100,000 "of the said yearly sum of one hundred and forty thousand pounds." *Cf.* p. 38.

[2] *Cf., i.a.,* Thorold Rogers, *l.c.,* p. 30, *sqq.*; Macleod, i., p. 452, *sqq.* ; de l'Hermitage, *Secret Correspondence,*

[3] See, *i.a.,* Rogers, *l.c.,* i., p. 32, *sqq.*

The minting of fresh coin was commenced in 1696, but proceeded at a slow pace. The consequences soon made themselves felt. As the date February 1, 1697, drew near, the scarcity of circulating medium became more accentuated.

The Exchequer Bills date from this period.

The Bank of England meanwhile had contented itself with receiving the light coins in circulation. It continued to do so. But as soon as the new coins made their appearance the Bank was compelled to pay its notes in coins of full weight. Apart from the fact that this operation inflicted a serious loss upon the Bank (5 ounces on every 12), this favourable opportunity was seized by its rivals to bring their antagonist down.

A few Goldsmiths combined, and succeeded in collecting bank-notes to the amount of £30,000, all of which they presented to the Bank for payment on May 5, 1697. The Directors refused payment, but continued to supply cash to their ordinary customers. Its enemies were greatly rejoicing in their success and believed themselves masters of the situations, but—owing to the publicity given to this incident by the Directors of the Bank—the ultimate result of the Goldsmiths' ruse was that public confidence was strengthened in the notes and that they continued to circulate.

Still, the storm had been allayed temporarily only, and the difficulties recurred. As a result of the continued scarcity of silver the Bank was, in the course of the same year, compelled to suspend cash payments against its notes. It announced that on all notes presented for payment 10 per cent. only of their face value would be paid in gold. Even at this rate it was unable to maintain payments of its notes and shortly afterwards the Bank paid them by instalments of 3 per cent.

Jealousy and competition manifested themselves under yet another form. The Government was in continual need of funds. This time it was the Tory party who proposed a scheme for the raising of £2,564,000 on condition that subscribers would be granted the privilege to found a Land Bank, viz., a bank which could issue notes on the security of landed property, and give credit at short notice on security which was more or less difficult of realisation.[1]

In spite of the opposition of the Bank and its friends, the Bill, after having been passed by Parliament, received the Royal Sanction in April, 1696,[2] and subscriptions were invited.

[1] A comparison of the scheme of Dr. Chamberlayne with that which Craddocke advocated 30 years previously, reveals a curious development of the idea during that period.

[2] The scheme had already been accepted in principle by the House of Commons in 1693. Its sponsors were Mr. Briscoe and Dr. Chamberlayne.

This was shortly after the above-mentioned run on the Bank of England. Either through the influence of its opponents or on account of the sound common-sense of the business men of those days, the public only subscribed an insignificant sum (£2,100), and the Land Bank disappeared from the financial stage almost before it had come into existence.

To the Bank of England this had been an object-lesson. It recognised that, if it were to justify its existence in the future, that existence had to be based upon something more substantial than a few clauses in a taxation bill. Originally the Bank had been created as a privilege granted for eleven years. Now it existed, and possessed vitality ; it formed a source of profit, and it rested with itself alone to prolong its life and to acquire a firm footing. Single handed this seemed impracticable. However, it had a powerful ally, the most powerful in a constitutional and parliamentary State, viz., the Government. Its endeavours to secure its position were favoured by the course of events.

The poor condition of the credit system and the Bank's own want of a greater working capital, together with the continual difficulties experienced by the Treasury in meeting State expenditure without unduly increasing taxation, made it possible for the Bank to obtain the fulfilment of its wishes. Twice it had borrowed from its shareholders, once already it had called up 20 per cent. of its sub- scribed capital, but apparently this did not suffice.[1]

In 1697 subscriptions were invited for addi- tional capital. The proceeds were to be handed over to the Government, as in 1694, as a loan at a rate of interest of 8 per cent. per annum. The additional capital was to rank *pari passu* with the original £1,200,000, and the new subscribers were to have the same rights as those enjoyed by the first stock- holders. The Bank was authorised to in- crease its working capital by a corresponding amount.

Whilst subscribers to the new capital were placed on the same footing as those who were already registered in the books of the Bank, new provisions were made with regard to the

[1] Of the original capital of £1,200,000, 60 per cent. only had been paid up, whilst the balance of 40 per cent. remained uncalled, by way of a reserve. That it was called up in 1696 and 1697 was due to the Bank's need of cash for the payment of its notes (Gilbart, i. p. 34). These payments of the balance of capital took place at the commencement of November, 1696, and of September, 1697. Their influence was clearly reflected in the quotations published by Rogers, although he refrains from referring to it. The loan of the 11th of June, 1696, which preceded the payment of the first instalment, was made by the shareholders themselves, in order that the Bank might not be obliged to call for payment in full of its shares. When it was nevertheless found necessary to have recourse to this, the loan was repaid out of proceeds of the call. Regarding the loan of the 15th of August, 1696, the Bank Books are silent.

notes which the Bank was going to issue over and above those already in circulation. They were to be payable at sight. Should payment be refused by the Bank, demand could be made to the Exchequer, who would pay the notes out of such funds as they might have outstanding in favour of the Bank, provided that such debt were due and irrespective of the interest of £100,000 which they paid annually to the Bank.[1]

The price which Parliament had to pay was embodied in the 28th clause of the Act 7 & 8 Wm. III. During the life of the Bank —viz., as long as the entire amount of its advance to the Government had not been repaid—it would enjoy an exclusive privilege, guaranteed by the State.[2]

[1] The result of this increase of capital, taken together with the successful recoinage, were soon perceptible. In the latter half of 1696, when the Bank only paid its notes by instalments of 3 per cent., they stood at a discount of from 8 to 18 per cent. In October, 1697, they were at par, and those which carried interest soon commanded a premium. The Exchequer Bills were similarly affected when it was provided that they were to be accepted at par in payment of taxes. The Government took advantage of this circumstance and reduced the rate of interest on these Bills to 4 per cent.

The payments of bank-notes to be made by the Exchequer may be compared in a measure to the system of the Venetian Banks, which, after 1526, were compelled to keep a balance of 500 ducats with the *provedatori supra banchi*, placed over them. It does not appear whether in London this provision has ever been put into practice. In Venice it was frequently acted upon.

[2] The subscription of 1697 only yielded £1,001,171 10s. This amount was repaid by the Government in 1707, but as

No other bank, so the provision ran, " or any other corporation, society, fellowship, company, or constitution in the nature of a bank, shall be erected or established, per-

this constituted a portion only of the sum advanced by the Bank to the Government, the privilege remained in force.

This repayment is connected with the history of the Act of 1697. The object of the Act was to provide the means required by the Government for the continuation of the war with France. The first difficulty was, however, that the Government were unable to meet their floating debt charges, which had accumulated to the amount of £5,160,459 14s. 9¼d. In order to meet these, in the first place, various taxes which had been granted in the times of the predecessors of William III., were continued to 1716, whilst others, which had already ceased to exist, were revived.

Secondly, the Government negotiated the above-mentioned loan with the Bank of England. Simultaneously with the expiration of the renewed taxes the loan became due. The deplorable condition of the Treasury, to which brief reference was made in the text, appears from the introductory remarks to this Act, " And whereas by reason of the *deficiencies of several of the aids, supplies, impositions, and duties above mentioned*, which *have not or will not be sufficient to answer the principal and interest charged thereupon*, and by reason of *the remoteness of the course of payment of the tallies and orders charged upon some of them*, and upon other the duties in this act before mentioned, *the owners of the said tallies* or orders are frequently *necessitated to sell and dispose thereof at great loss, or at an excessive discount* whereby the *publick credit* is very much *prejudiced* and *impaired*, and *the trade* and *other publick and private affairs* with this realm *do exceedingly suffer;* and whereas it is imputed or estimated that *the deficiencies or sums, which are or will be wanting to satisfy and pay off all principal and interest* due or to be due on the deficient aids, duties, or funds before mentioned (over and above *all arrears*, standing out upon any of them, which are determined and over and above all monies to be raised by such of them as are yet expired) do or may amount to the sums following . . ." &c. (See *Statutes at Large*, Part X. pp. 37, 38. The italics are by the author.)

mitted, suffered, countenanced, or allowed by Act of Parliament within this kingdom."

When the Bill which contained these provisions received the Royal Sanction the existence of the Bank was assured.

The Act of 1697 was again an act of ways and means, in which eighteen clauses only (20—37) dealt with the Bank of England. But it was no longer the question of ways and means to which the attention of the Government was exclusively directed. Paragraph 20 commenced : " And for the better restoring of credit of the nation and advancing the credit of the Corporation of the Governor and Company, or the Bank of England, be it enacted . . ." &c.

The usefulness of the Bank had been recognised. The valuable assistance which it had rendered to the King during his campaign on the Continent had demonstrated how important it was to possess an institution of this kind and to safeguard its stability. The Bank had learnt its lessons during the first years of its existence, and the Government had recognised during the grave monetary crisis of those years that above all State credit should be maintained undisturbed. Thus circumstances have from the outset made England the country of a banking monopoly. The first step necessarily led to the second. Eleven years afterwards, before the expiration of the privilege, the issue of notes in England and Wales was virtually limited to the Bank.

Various endeavours were made to establish similar private institutions. A Charitable Corporation Fund was started in 1705, but failed through mismanagement. Another competitor of greater importance was the Mine Adventurers Company of England, who, under the management of Sir Humphrey Mackworth, issued bank-notes and carried on banking business.

The Bank of England knew, however, the weak side of the Government. Whilst, on the one hand, they had, in 1707, repaid part of the Bank's capital, they, on the other hand, borrowed afresh £2,500,000 from the Bank in the succeeding year (1708), and in consideration inserted in the new Bank Charter a clause granting to the Bank of England the monopoly of joint stock banking business.

This Act was also an act of Ways and Means, but this time the first part of it was concerned with provisions regarding the increase of the Bank's capital. Act 7 Anne, c. 7, " An Act for enlarging the capital stock of the Bank of England, and for raising a further supply to her Majesty . . ." &c. By this Act it is provided : " That during the continuance of the said corporation of the Governor and Company of the Bank of England, it shall not be lawful for any body politic or corporate whatsoever, created or to be created (other than the said Governor and Company of the Bank of England), or for any other persons whatsoever, united or to be united in covenants or partnership, exceeding the number of six persons, in that part of Great Britain called England, to borrow, owe, or take up any sum or sums of money on their bills or notes payable at demand, or at a less time than six months from the borrowing thereof."

It is always exceedingly difficult to word an Act in such a way as to provide absolute safeguards against evasion of its spirit. In this case, too, it was mooted by many that a possibility of evasion existed, and towards the expiration of the Bank Charter (1742) various methods were tried to bring these ideas into practice. The Bank was only too apprehensive lest these endeavours might be successful, and when, in the above-mentioned year, it secured the extension of its Charter in consideration of a loan of £1,600,000, it succeeded in having the Bank monopoly accurately defined in Act 10 and 11 George II., c. 13 (par. 5).

Having secured this, it considered itself safe against any competition.[1]

---

[1] Macleod in his *Theory and Practice of Banking* ably exposes the error of the Bank. If the Bank had adhered to the sober meaning of the words in the Act of 1697 that "no other Bank or

With this Act the Bank reached the zenith of its power. From a mere instrument in the hands of the Government for the supply of money it had developed into a powerful ally, but at the same time a shrewd tyrant, who knew the failings of its master and managed always to have its own way.

From that date it declined. Freed from competition, it ignored the signs of the times, and when the Government began to feel stronger, the Bank's close relations with it made it an easy tool in the hands of the Ministry. This stage in its history will be dealt with in a subsequent chapter.

PART II

It may be assumed that with the establishment of the Bank of England a new era in the

any other Corporation . . . in the nature of a Bank shall be erected," it would have prevented any other part of the banking business, which, in 1742, was already known to its full extent, from being exercised separately from a method of debt transfer, which at that time was looked upon as indissolubly connected with banking, because it formed its most remunerative branch.

Macleod goes too far when he states that in the eighteenth century banking "merely implied the issue of bank-notes." The written documents which date from that period certainly disprove this hypothesis. Banking was, and continued to be, the transmission of capital from one party to another, but the bank-notes formed the principal means of transfer. The Bank of England thought that by prohibiting others from using this means of transfer it had deprived them of the means of carrying on banking business. This was shortsighted, but was no proof that the Bank did not understand its business.

development of the English credit system began. Although it is true that the Goldsmiths developed into bankers within a comparatively short time, it may, with a fair measure of certainty, be stated that their notes (including their promissory notes) continued to be based on funds placed on deposit with them. Some doubt may be felt on this subject, but the special way in which the Bank of England was authorised to carry on business is so emphatically laid down in the Act of 1694 that there seems sufficient reason to regard the year of the Bank's foundation as inaugurating a new era.[1]

First of all the Bank's business methods must be reviewed. They consisted on the debit side of—

1. The receipt of deposits.

2. The issue of bank-notes (promissory notes).

[1] This view is supported by the author of the pamphlet *A Brief Account of the Intended Bank of England* (probably Wm. Patterson), in which he states, in conclusion, that the opposition to his pamphlet must not be wondered at, "as being the common fate of all good and generous undertakings, that are, or ever were, in this world, the nature of men being bent against everything which they fancy innovation. . . . that none knows or at least ought to know more than they, as out of a natural unbelief and suspicion of all they cannot see." We may also refer to the reply to this pamphlet : *Some useful reflections upon a Pamphlet called A Brief Account of the Intended Bank of England*, probably from the pen of Dr. Chamberlayne, in which the author reproaches the advocate of the Bank of England *inter alia* with having stolen the idea of granting credit in this form from the doctor himself.

1. It will be readily understood that depositors demanded for their balance with the Bank a voucher of which they could dispose by means of cheques or otherwise. Curiously enough, the facilities allowed for this purpose to its depositors by the Bank of England were almost identical with the methods followed in mediæval times by the Venetian Banks (*Contadi di banco*). Regarding these *Contadi di banco* Goldschmidt says [1] : " It is not clear whether they were cheques, independent deposit receipts, or mere copies of book-entries (*partidæ*)." As far as the Bank of England was concerned the form of these vouchers can be positively ascertained.

At the very first meeting of the Directors of the Bank of England it was resolved that three methods of " giving receipts for running cashes " should be followed :—

1. " To give out Running Cash Notes and to endorse on them what is paid off in part " (independent deposit receipts).

2. " To keep an account with yᵉ Creditor in a Book or paper of his owne " (mere copies of book entries, *partidæ*).

3. " By charging [2] Notes on the Bank, to accept notes drawn on yᵉ Bank " (cheques).

The latter method apparently corresponds with the cheque system of the present day, and

[1] *Universal Geschichte des Handselrechts*, p. 324.
[2] Changing ?

may be considered similar to the Venetian *Contadi di banco*. A receipt was handed to the customer for the amount of his balance with the Bank, of which sum he could dispose at any time by drawing on the Bank. This receipt bore the name of " note accountable," and in virtue of such notes the Bank declared itself willing " to accept notes drawn on ye Bank."

In the case of each of these three systems we have to deal with deposit receipts which were issued by the Bank itself. On all three the amounts were written which the customer was credited and debited with, that is to say, in the case of Nos. 1 and 3, by stating on the receipt itself how much had been withdrawn at various times, and in the case of No. 2, in the usual way in which the entries were also made in the books of the Bank.

This is deducible from the form set out in the first Minutes kept by the Board of Directors of the Bank of England of a " Note Accountable," viz. :—

LONDON, [date]

Received of   [name of customer]   a sum of
[amount   ]
Current mony
for which I promise to be accountable.
ye particulars of the note,
as to repayment, etc.

(Signature)

The difference between (1) " Running Cash Notes " and (3) " Notes Accountable " consisted in the transferability of the " Running Cash Note." Whenever the holder of a " Note Accountable " (depositor in account current) disposed of parts of the amount standing to his credit by means of cheques, the cheques themselves were honoured, but the sums so drawn were written off on the note. The same applied to the second deposit receipt, (2) the book.

The " Note Accountable " remained in the hands of the depositor in the same way as the " deposit receipt No. 2." Against it the cheque circulated. In the case of the " running cash notes " it was the cash note itself which circulated.

As the Running Cash Note was easily transferable there was not so great a necessity for following the same procedure in its case as with the " note accountable." But when part of the balance was withdrawn in specie by the depositor or the endorsee this amount was written down on the document which had to be presented to the Bank for the purpose of withdrawing a part or the whole of the deposit itself.

At the Bank of England one document only relating to this method of keeping cash has survived the ravages of time and has been preserved in a somewhat damaged, yet sufficiently legible, condition. It is a " Note Accountable " which reads as follows :—

LONDON, ye 10th June 1697.

Received of Capt Bas^{il} [   ] Percey a [   ]
forty seaven pounds five shilling
Current mony
for which I promise to be accountable [   ]
demand

     * * * * *¹)   For the [   ]
     * * * *   Of the [   ]

Otherwise the proofs themselves are no longer in existence. Yet the above-mentioned provisions, derived from so reliable a source, are none the less of importance. The more so, if we consider that the Bank of England, though founded on the same principle as the three Continental Banks (Amsterdam, Genoa, and Venice), was at the same time closely connected with the peculiar Goldsmiths trade which had developed at home.[2]

The " Note Accountable " is the only documentary evidence of the fact that the Bank of England from the outset adopted the cheque system, which was then already in vogue. Further data are not available. In the books of the Bank of England for the first eight years of its existence the word cheque is never mentioned, nor is it possible to deduce from other records with any

---

[1] The words and figures written here are illegible.
[2] Cf. inter alia, Rogers, loc. cit., p. 9.

degree of certainty, that such a system was in use.

The " Note Accountable," as we have seen, represents a cheque contract *in optima forma*. The Note itself is a deposit receipt. It constitutes evidence of a claim on the Bank which the party named in the note could enforce. If the latter disposed of part of this sum by requesting the Bank to pay over a certain amount to the taker of his cheque or bill, such cheque or bill once having been paid by the Bank and being in its possession, discharges its responsibility and constitutes counter evidence against the claim of the customer in virtue of the deposit. The sum repaid is written off on the " Note Accountable " and the evidence of payment, already in existence as far as the Bank is concerned, has thus been transferred to this Note also. The cheque or bill may then be cancelled if desired.

The holder of the cheque does not derive any title to the deposit from that document itself. A cession of right has not taken place.[1]

To the holder, the cheque or bill merely represents evidence of a request addressed by the depositor to the Bank. Even in case of

---

[1] If a cession had taken place, both the depositor, on his Note Accountable, and the holder of the cheque or bill, in virtue of such cheque or bill, could make the same claim against the Bank, which is hardly reconcilable with proper legal principles.

acceptance the holder will have a claim on the Bank alone, not on the funds deposited with the Bank by the holder of the " Note Account-able " (drawer of the cheque).

At first the Bank of England was, above all, a deposit Bank.[1]

This is apparent from the very first arrange-ments made by the Directors. I might almost say from the very first document dealing with the basis on which they were prepared to transact business, viz., the regulations which they laid down as to how to keep an account with their customers, and the documents whereby they decided to carry them out.

A few months after the Bank commenced business it was decided that it should not dis-count for nor grant loans to parties who did not keep their cash there. This stipulation was made for the sake of security, but was revoked and restored again on several occa-sions, especially in the days when the English monetary system was in a chaotic state.[2]

Even after this condition was finally aban-doned, preference continued to be shown to

[1] Rogers, who otherwise so concisely and lucidly describes the Bank of England of those days, does not, in my opinion, sufficiently emphasise this fact. From subsequent paragraphs on pages 5, 66, and 136 of his work it appears that he holds the same view.

[2] Rogers' assumption that the Bank did not begin to discount bills until a few weeks after its incorporation is incorrect. The Bank books prove that a very few days after its establishment such operations had already begun.

customers (depositors) as distinct from outsiders.

Nevertheless, from the outset, the Bank was considered in many quarters to be a note-issuing bank, pure and simple. This view was presumably based on the fact that ere long its development proceeded entirely on those lines. This has already briefly been commented upon at the close of the first chapter. Before reverting to this question at greater length, it is proposed first to deal with No. 2 of its "Debit Operations," viz., the Bank-notes.

2. The Bank of England, under its Charter, was authorised to issue notes, "bills under the common seal, sealed bills," [1] as they were called, to an amount not exceeding its subscribed capital. The capital itself was to be handed over to the Government and the working capital had to be found by the receipt of deposits and by the issue of notes. Instead of following this line the Bank paid over to the Government the amount of the subscribed capital in "sealed Bank Bills," but retained as working capital the sums paid up in cash on these subscriptions, viz., 60 per cent. [2] of the total sums subscribed.

---

[1] The "Sealed Bill," as the name indicates, was a Bill of Exchange (*Trockner Wechsel*), on which the seal of the Bank was impressed. The Bank undertook to pay to a party expressly named therein, at a certain specified time, a certain specified sum of money.

[2] See Luttrell's *Diary*, August 1, 1694.

The advantage of this transaction is apparent. The Government paid to the Bank, say, from 4 to 8 per cent.[1] on the capital so received, whilst the Bank allowed from 3 to $4\frac{1}{2}$ per cent. on its notes. The Bank received interest on its capital at rates ranging from 1 to 5 per cent. without having to part with it. When the " bills " returned to the Bank through the creditors of the Government, they were, as a rule, exchanged against new " Bank Bills " or occasionally against " Running Cash Notes." In the latter case the Bank induced these creditors to leave at least a portion of their cash on deposit with the Bank. At the same time the Bank retained the disposal of £720,000, which sum was available for its own operations.

Hardly had the entire amount been remitted to the Government, when the Bank decided to make another issue of notes to replace the old ones when these should return from circulation. In this way the turnover during the first years of its existence amounted to £2,400,000.

The Bank Directors were fully aware of the importance of such action. The profit-earning capacity of the Bank could be greatly enhanced if means could be devised whereby the note issue might be extended beyond the legal maximum of £1,200,000. At the end of

[1] Adam Smith, *Wealth of Nations*, v. ch. iii.

April, 1695, a committee was appointed to consult with the Bank's legal advisers, and to consider whether the prohibition mentioned in the Act placed unsurmountable obstacles in the way of the realisation of this idea. The Committee soon issued its report. Its conclusion was that the wording of the Charter did not admit of the issue of " Sealed Bills " to a larger amount.

However, if not by direct, the object in view might be attained by circuitous means. The essentials of " Sealed Bills " were the Seal,[1] the name of the person in whose favour it was drawn and the time which the promissory note had to run.

If one or more of these *essentialia* were omitted, a document might be created which would no longer be a " Sealed Bill," and the law placed no obstacles in the way of the issue of such paper.

A decision was taken in accordance herewith. On May 1, 1695, the Bank of England created its promissory notes to bearer, at sight, and without seal. The impression of the seal was placed at the top of the document.

The notes were printed. Only the amount and date of issue were left blank, to be filled in by the cashiers of the Bank, in writing,

---

[1] The Seal, not the signature, bestowed the legal sanction upon a contract. This principle dated back to a time when the art of writing was an accomplishment not generally met with.

for fixed sums of £5, £10, £15, £20, £30, £40, £50, and £100. At the same time each series was provided with a watermark, ranging from A to H.

These " Lettered Notes " marked an important step forward, and it is doubtful whether their issue would not have caused the Bank to develop along different lines than those actually followed, but circumstances did not favour the new notes.

" Lettered Notes " to an amount of about £200,000 were printed. On June 15th they were put into circulation. Two months later it was decided to withdraw them. The absence of the Bank's seal and the fact that they were payable to bearer [1] were features which made the temptation to forge them too strong for advocates of the maxim, " Make money by all means, honestly if you can, only make it."

The genuine notes gradually returned from circulation, and no further attempt at a fresh issue was made.[2]

As far as we know, the Bank has never renewed its experiments in this direction, and

[1] The notes to order had to be endorsed and, apart from the safeguard which the relation with the customer offered to the Bank, every additional signature rendered its imitation more difficult. Probably the state of the coinage at the time presented another reason for their withdrawal.

[2] In all 4,500 notes representing an aggregate total of £125,000 were put in circulation.

the " Sealed Bank Bills " have, with a single modification, passed into the bank-note of this century.

Prior to the experiment above referred to the Bank had begun to place its Running Cash Notes on the same basis as the Sealed Bills. The balance of the £1,200,000 was remitted to the Government in such notes ; previously it had issued Sealed Bills and Running Cash Notes indiscriminately when discounting bills of exchange and Goldsmiths' notes. Before the close of 1694 both kinds of notes were merged into one under the name of Bank-note.

This need not excite surprise. The " notes for Running Cash " were deposit receipts, and in practice it is immaterial whether a borrowing operation is carried out by the issue of a promissory note which may be enforced at any time, or by the creation of a deposit which may be withdrawn at any time. In both cases the Bank, by discounting bills of exchange with either of its Notes, gives future against future capital.[1] In giving a Running Cash Note the Bank issued a document in evidence of having created a deposit in favour of the person who discounted the Bill.[2]

[1] Both kinds of transactions still take place at the present time. The documentary evidence of the deposit however, has, in the course of time, been dropped and the public content themselves with the double entry in the books of the Bank.

[2] Reference might be made to what Goldschmidt (*Univ. Gesch.*,

Although the Bank placed both on the same footing, it was hardly possible that both should circulate with equal freedom. The Running Cash Notes had the advantage of being payable at sight,[1] but they were at a disadvantage in so far as they were issued in odd amounts, and, though transferable, could not easily pass from hand to hand. These disadvantages were sufficient to free the "Sealed Bills" from any risk of being elbowed out, and after the experiment with the "Lettered Notes" proved so absolute a failure their supremacy was assured beyond doubt. At the same time the experiment demonstrated that the Bank of England was alive to the great importance of a note circulation. This partly explains the readiness with which the Bank accepted at every renewal of its Charter any suggestion regarding the extension of its share capital, for it involved the extension of a very remunerative source of income.

True, on one subsequent occasion the Bank issued a special description of notes, viz., the so-called "specie-notes," but these were in

p. 320) says of the *fedi de deposito* of the old Italian Banks: "These were either promissory notes or vouchers certifying that a certain amount had been placed to the credit of an account in the books of the Bank . . . . both kinds of receipts circulate instead of cash. . . . Primitive Bank-notes."

[1] The "Sealed Bills" were mostly payable at six months and were discounted. In 1697 it was enacted that they should be payable "at demand." From that time they bear interest at the rate of 2d. *per diem.*

7

reality only " Running Cash Notes," pure and simple, with the additional proviso that they had to be issued against deposits of heavy coin and be repaid in the same way.[1]

This was, however, merely a temporary experiment, during the period from 1696 to 1698, and was abandoned as soon as the new coinage was completed.

Meanwhile the Bank modified its way of doing business according to circumstances. The difficulties in connection with the change in the coinage compelled the Bank to devise means for the avoidance of specie payments. Even at this time customers were allowed to effect payments by transfer in the books of the Bank.[2]

A few years later, in 1698, facilities were made for the Bank's customers to dispose of their balances by means of cheques. The Bank opened a " Drawing Account," on which the customers were credited not only with the amount of their payments in cash, but also with the amounts paid on bills which had matured, and later with the sums for which bills had been discounted.[3]

---

[1] See Luttrell's *Diary*, July 16, 1696, and Rogers, *loc. cit.*, p. 66.

[2] " Such as think fit, for their convenience, to keep an account in a book with the Bank, may transfer any sum under five pounds from his own to another man's account " (Gilbart, i. p. 34).

[3] This happened at the same time that the Bank decided to cease allowing interest on Running Cash Notes, that is to say, on

From this it might have been expected that, after the failure of its experiment in 1695, and having once adopted this course, the Bank would have based its credit system mainly on deposits. This it did not. By degrees the issue of bank-notes assumed greater proportions, and at the end of the period under review the Bank of England was without doubt mainly a note-issuing bank.

The exact course of this development is still shrouded in mystery. Very likely the bank-books, and especially the resolutions passed by the Directors of the Bank at their Board Meetings, would throw much light on this subject, and, generally speaking, on the events of the last decade of the seventeenth century. When it is once generally recognised that the eighteenth century belongs to the domain of history, the veil which still hangs over one of the most interesting and least explored periods of English banking history will be lifted by the Bank of England itself, and that august institution will follow the example set by private bankers in the provinces by throwing open its valuable records for scientific research. For the present there is no alternative but to confine oneself—more or less—to suppositions which, of course, are made entirely without prejudice.

deposits. This system, still adhered to, is thus vindicated by its antiquity.

As soon as the difficulties experienced during the first few years of the Bank's existence had been overcome, and it was no longer necessary for the Directors to concentrate their energies on the maintenance of their institution, their successive resolutions display remarkable uniformity. The latter part of 1698 and the years 1699 and 1700 were wholly taken up with administrative measures regarding fresh issues of Bank Bills, their repayment and cancellation.

The credit operations carried on by the Bank consisted chiefly in the discounting of Treasury Tallies and the granting of advances to the Government on the security of the taxes.[1]

As a commercial undertaking it would have had to be content with considerably smaller profits, competition in that direction being so much more severe. In addition to this the large sums required by the successive Governments of William III. and Queen Anne proved sufficient to satisfy three commercial institutions.[2]

In 1782 the permanent debt of the Bank amounted to £11,000,000, to which sum it

[1] For the various methods of borrowing followed by the Government, see Phillipovich von Philipsberg ; *Die Bank von England* &c., c. ii., No. 2, p. 72 ; also Adam Smith, *Wealth of Nations*, v., ch. iii.

[2] The East India Company, the Bank of England, and the South Sea Company.

had grown from £1,200,000 in 1694. Until 1727 interest at 8 to 4 per cent. was paid thereon, and it was not until thirty years later that the interest paid by the Government was reduced to 3 per cent.

The floating debt was far in excess of this amount, and since 1701 the Bank of England was the only intermediary (with the exception of the South Sea Company during a very brief period) between the Government and its subjects. On this debt likewise interest at the rate of 4 per cent. was paid.

In addition thereto the anticipation of practically all the taxes constituted a remunerative operation, and it will thus be readily understood why the Bank preferred such transactions to the changeable and less profitable business of supplying merchants and industrial undertakings with capital. Moreover, periods of war are seldom conducive to the development of trade and industry.

The Bank supplied capital to the Government in the shape of " sealed Bills." In this way the Bank was enabled, even when no deposits were received, to transfer capital from the hands of the public into the Treasury.

It is probable that gradually the amount of deposits decreased.[1]

---

[1] In 1696 the amount of Running Cash Notes in circulation was only slightly inferior to that of the Sealed Bank Bills, viz. £764,169 10s. 6d., against £893,000 respectively.

Since 1699 the Bank had ceased to allow interest on funds deposited with it (Running Cash Notes). Where the Bank itself was used by the Government for the marketing of its floating debt (Treasury Bills, Lottery Tickets, &c., securities which yielded a high rate of interest), it would indeed have been surprising if the public had continued to entrust its available cash to the Bank and thus allowed it to secure profits, which they might easily obtain themselves.

The keeping of "accounts current" with the Bank on the basis of the conditions fixed in 1698 likewise met with scant encouragement on the part of private persons. In the first place the severe competition which prevailed, exercised a prejudicial effect. The private bankers received no protection at the hands of the Government. To them, therefore, it was of paramount importance to secure the goodwill of the general public in London. If only they contented themselves with a lower rate of interest than that paid by the Government, they were sure to free themselves from the competition of the Bank of England.

Considerable amounts were entrusted to them, consisting of the cash resources of various persons : money in account current. Yet, during this period, this was not accompanied by a corresponding extension of the method of transfer based on such deposits.

The way in which cash was kept by the Goldsmiths has already been referred to. With them the "Running Cash Note" originated, the deposit receipt which the Bank of England so readily adopted.[1]

They were familiar with the promissory note and the cheque. The Running Cash Note gradually disappeared from circulation in the same way as it did with the Bank of England, probably as a result of the cumbersome process of transfer, either of the note itself (if this was at all possible) or of the available balance mentioned therein. The same circumstances must, I think, be held responsible for the fact that the public showed a decided preference for the "promissory notes" over the cheques. The note better answered the requirements of a circulating medium, as it could change hands without formalities. In addition to this, the security offered by the note was considered superior to that of the cheque. The payment of a note was guaranteed by a well-known firm, while the ultimate payment of a cheque depended solely upon the balance of any given citizen with a banker, which might at any time be subject to severe fluctuation. The fact that the use of cheques never assumed large proportions, not-

---

[1] Very probably they carried interest at the same rate as their *bills*. Why, otherwise, did the Bank of England from the outset allow the same interest on both?

withstanding the introduction of the " account current " system by the Bank of England, should be attributed to the same cause or similar causes. The Government likewise received its advances in the shape of bills. This method of granting credit enabled the Bank to ascertain at all times the amount advanced to the Government, and to retain in its hands the power of exercising a certain supervision over these loans.[1]

Its close relations with the Treasury was one of the reasons why until 1759 the smallest denomination of its bank-notes was £20, whilst private bankers issued notes for smaller amounts. The Acts of 1775 and 1777 [2] further contributed to the development of the cheque system.

In addition to these reasons of utility, the Act of 1705 placed the promissory note on exactly the same basis, from a legal point of view, as a bill of exchange.

It is not necessary to attempt to estimate the relative importance of these two causes, or to explain their connection with one another,

---

[1] The Government never received the amount demanded in a lump sum, but drew upon its balance as, and when, it was required for expenditure.

[2] These Acts prohibited for a certain period the issue of notes below a certain amount. By Act 15 Geo. III. c. 15 the limit was fixed at £1 and in 1777 by Act 17 Geo. III. c. 30 at £5. In 1787 these Acts were renewed for an indefinite period, but in 1797 they were suspended.

especially as so few historical data are available regarding the actual extension of this circulating medium.

It is now, however, possible to understand why, when the cheque became more and more prominent in the ordinary course of business transactions, the Bank of England looked upon this development with equanimity. Its own sphere of activity was not interfered with. Long since it had ceased to be chiefly a deposit bank, and its note circulation was extended thereby. It gave the Bank a virtual monopoly.

The little information which is available is nevertheless sufficient to reconstruct the character of the circulating medium, which originated in the seventeenth century, and continues in existence at the present day without having suffered any essential modification.

The resemblance between the English and the Italian (especially the Venetian) banking systems, as far as their historical development is concerned, is an undeniable and important factor.

In the first place a comparison of the two systems renders it possible to understand and supplement phenomena, in themselves difficult of explanation. For the Goldsmiths did not invent a new business. They only continued the profession which before their time had been carried on by the Jews, and especially the Lombards.

A comparative study may lead us still further. Banking in England only began to develop when the Venetian system had already run the whole course of its history. For that reason Venice cannot have exercised a direct influence on London. When at some future date all sources of information have been brought to light, it may become apparent how, under substantially identical circumstances, the same idea followed the same course of development though neither system exercised an influence on the other ; and how, when the circumstances changed, when liberty of action was granted to one and withheld from the other, subsequent development led to such widely divergent issues.

With both the deposit formed the basis.[1]

[1] The *depositum regulare* may be left out of consideration. When the "banchieri" began to develop in Italy this form of deposit had been superseded. See Goldschmidt, *Univ. Gesch.*, p. 319, and the authors quoted by him.

The Lombards in London also no longer used this form. The custom of depositing funds for safe-keeping in convents and the Mint, in vogue during the intervening period, may be compared to the practice of building fireproof safes, and offering to the public the opportunity of hiring such safes (Safe Deposit Companies). It would be interesting to know what proportion of the money thus deposited for safe custody was received from parties who acted as intermediaries, and had in their turn accepted deposits from others. At the time of the suspension of payments by the Exchequer during the reign of Charles II. such deposits probably made up the bulk of the total amount.

Of the items forming the deposit a list was made. The list served the depositor as a voucher.

The first development of this list was the " Running Cash Note." Although not a single one of these documents has been preserved for posterity, their form may be deduced from the specimen of the " Note Accountable " of the Bank of England, which is still in existence. This deduction is based on two hypotheses.

Firstly : the form of the " Note Accountable " has been expressly defined in the Minutes of the Board Meetings held by the Directors of the Bank of England.[1] It was a new departure. Why otherwise should (1) a special form have been prepared for this document and not for the " Running Cash Note," and (2) this specified form have been mentioned in the Minutes?

It is conceivable that in determining its form the Directors adhered as much as possible to what existed already, and were guided by the " Running Cash Note." In this way a novelty introduced by them would most likely find favour with the public.

Secondly, as has already been pointed out, the wording of the " Running Cash Notes " was copied by the Bank of England from those issued by the Goldsmiths.

[1] See p. 55.

These notes would then have run as follows :

London, y^e

Received *of* . . . .
Y^e summe of . . . .
(*Current mony*)
Which I promise to pay on demand.

(*Y^e particulars* (Signature)
of the note, as to
repayment etc.)

It was a deposit receipt, pure and simple, with promise to pay, evidence of the contract of account current between banker and depositor. To the " Running Cash Note " of a subsequent period the " order " clause was added.[1]

If the theory be not too hazardous, it may be suggested that the " promissory note " owes its origin to these notes. It is easy to suppose that gradually the reference to the account-current contract was omitted and that the promissory note became a simple undertaking on the part of the banker to pay a certain person, or his order (for the sake of negotiability)—afterwards to bearer—a certain specified sum of money.[2]

[1] Frequent reference is made in the books of Backwell to the fact that several notes were simultaneously presented for payment by one person, and that in return for these notes one single note was issued to him for the whole amount. The notes presented by the customer were not all signed by himself.

[2] The Bank of England was the first to issue notes in fixed amounts.

The probability that the development of the promissory note has proceeded on these lines is increased by a comparison with the origin of the cheque.[1]

The cheque was evidence of a request addressed by the depositor to the banker on the strength of the annexed list (proof of the account current) and this request was made in writing for the sake of convenience, in order to avoid the depositor's personal attendance at such transaction.

The banker in his turn proceeded in the same way. Instead of giving a long specified account of the balance which he had in hand he gave a short statement of part (or the whole) of the funds deposited with him, and added to it a promise to pay.

In the one case we have a list plus a request, in the other an (abbreviated) list plus a promise. If the list be omitted, and the evidence of the account-current contract [2] be withheld, the plain cheque and the bank-note remain.[3]

If this deduction be correct it will be under-

---

[1] See Chapter I., Part 2, p. 54 and following.

[2] *Cf.* p. 111 and following.

[3] It is not until later that the " Running Cash Note " as such became superfluous, and probably it merged into the form of the " deposit receipt " of the present day, by which the funds deposited are not entered in account current, but have to be withdrawn in their entirety. Gilbart, *Theory of Banking*, i. p. 131.

stood why, in English law, legal provisions similar to those applicable to Bills of Exchange are applicable to cheques and promissory notes ; the law looks upon the cheque as a bill which wants acceptance, and on the promissory note as the acceptance of a bill which has practically still to be drawn.

The latter characteristic is still more clearly revealed in the " Note Accountable " of the Bank of England, which is now entirely obsolete, and which has presumably been supplanted by the " drawing account " of the present time.[1]

With the " Note Accountable " the Banker handed to the future drawer the proof of his undertaking to honour all requests for payment addressed to him in proper manner, up to the amount named in the document.[2]

The book, instituted by the Bank of England at its foundation, and of which no further mention is made in the Minute books previously referred to, is probably identical with the modern " pass-book." [3] Probably, at first, all transactions between the Bank and its customer were entered therein immediately after they had taken place.

Later, presumably, these transactions were,

[1] The "drawing account" was kept in the books of the banker, and formed, with these books, evidence of the contract entered into between the banker and his customer.

[2] " To accept notes drawn on Ye bank," p. 86.

[3] *Cf.* p. 56, *note.*

for the sake of convenience, entered at certain fixed periods and became mere copies of what had already been entered in the books of the bank. At the present time the holders are still requested, in order to afford some means of control, to hand in these pass-books once every quarter in order that the various items may be entered up in conformity with the books of the bank.[1]

Here again the entire proof of the transaction is contained in the books of the banking institutions.

The development of the credit system since the establishment of the Bank of England is characterised by the combination of two transactions, viz., the granting and the receiving of credit, which were formerly dealt with separately, but are now performed at one and the same time.

The Bank uses future capital as a basis for its banking operations. It supplies future capital in exchange for future capital, and *vice versâ.* Bills are discounted and notes given in exchange ; " loans " are granted against security and their amount paid in notes or placed to the credit of the borrower in account current. When a bill falls due or the term for which the loan was granted ex-

---

[1] The pass-book is not filled in by the holders themselves, as, according to Kuhlenbech, *Der Check*, seems to be customary in Germany.

pires, the repayment takes place in notes of the bank itself. Instead of acting as intermediary between depositor and borrower the Bank becomes the intermediary between those possessed of capital (in the shape of future capital) on the one hand, and itself on the other. He who discounts a Bill with the Bank, receives in exchange an amount of present capital which he deposits again with the same bank. In return he receives a promissory note of the same bank which entitles him at all times to the receipt of the amount due to him.

Of this right he does not avail himself. He transfers the promissory note to a third party in payment of goods delivered or services rendered. Thereby the Bank is again placed between two parties, of whom one constantly changes. The promissory note circulates until it returns to the place of issue either as a deposit or in payment of a claim which has fallen due.

In fact, the transaction is of a twofold character. The person who supplies future capital to the Bank receives present capital in exchange. He leaves this, however, with the Bank, and thus provides it with present capital and receives future capital in exchange. While the future capital which he provided in the first instance is inconvertible for the present, he receives this time future capital which may be converted into present capital at any time by demand made at the Bank, that is to say, of which the time when it becomes due has not been fixed at a certain date. He receives a claim which can be enforced at any time and which—for the sake of brevity—I will call *short future capital*. The best illustration of this is afforded by book credits (moneys at call).

Those who formerly deposited present capital with the Bank may now give " short future capital " (bank-note or cheque) and receive present capital in return, leave this on deposit with the Bank, and in exchange take either short future capital likewise repayable at any time though in different form (note for a cheque, book balance for notes), or *long future capital* productive of interest, and redeemable at a date to be agreed upon beforehand (deposit).

Only the actual transfer of present capital is eliminated.

The consequent extension of the banking system has already been briefly referred to. Whilst formerly only one form of capital, viz., the cash deposits, formed the basis of the Bank's operations, now the future capital which has been lent to the Bank by its customers, also forms a basis of the credit transaction which takes place between them.

The working capital of the Bank is increased with the total amount of all sums granted on credit by the Bank.[1]

Thus the Bank may continue to carry on credit operations as long as the public is willing to deal with it. The Bank has no limit, as long as A deposits again whatever A withdraws, and *vice versâ*. The one essential is that notes and book credits should remain in circulation until the bill discounted with them falls due, or until the loan granted through their means is repaid.[2]

Considerations of time limit the operations of the banker.

This extension of the banking system leaves the old branches of the trade intact. The banks continue to receive present capital (cash) and also to supply it. In order to be able to supply cash they are obliged to keep a certain reserve in hand.

It might otherwise appear as if the transfer of actual cash had been relegated to the background. This appearance must be avoided, in order not to create the impression which

[1] Those who accept notes in payment grant credit in the shape of present against future capital. In fact, as long as book credits and notes circulate, the entire amount of capital represented thereby benefits the credit system through the intervention of the Bank, without ever having been in its possession.

[2] On condition, of course, that the community be able to await the completion of the various processes of production without its ordinary requirements being left unprovided for.

many outsiders seem to entertain, that the money market is a place where only financial paper is dealt in, " credits," as it is termed in practice.

The result would be an incorrect representation of the actual condition of affairs. It would appear as if the banks no longer acted as intermediaries, but themselves created the capital which they supply to others.

This is not the case.[1] But owing to that close connection with each other,[2] due to the development of commerce, to the greater reliability in the administration of justice, and to the fact that the Banks are known throughout the country, they are in a position to rely upon the expectation that credit will be extended to them at all times. As soon as experience has taught them that their notes (afterwards their book credits) circulate for a certain time, and that, in exchange for future capital falling due within this period of circulation, they can give their " short future capital " repayable at any time, the Banks need no longer confine themselves to the present capital which they receive from depositors, but all capital of whatever nature

---

[1] This becomes more apparent, if viewed from a legal standpoint. Most payments and transfers of capital in London take place by means of cheques. It would hardly be justifiable to regard payment by cheque as equivalent to the cession of a claim.

[2] Especially with regard to the Banks in Scotland,

which is entrusted to them becomes a basis for their credit operations.

It will be instructive to compare the banking struggle in London with that in Scotland. Although the Bank of England soon realised the great advantage of those business methods, it must have recognised at the same time that a new principle can only gain ground if based upon what preceded it, and since the new grew out of the old it should continue to make one whole with it until it gradually forces the old into the background of history and itself, in its turn, forms the basis of other new ideas.

The newly developed banking business could only be undertaken by those who issued fiduciary circulating medium or who were concerned with the system of accounts current. The future capital issued by them must remain in circulation, and their notes must be accepted in payment by a number of persons. Thus a Bank obtains a wider sphere of activity. It no longer needs to defer the conclusion of a transaction with a borrower until it is provided with present capital. The party who accepts the Bank's notes from its customers takes the place of the depositor.

Of course, this can only be achieved if the Bank counts among its customers all, or at any rate a considerable number, of the members of the business community in a particular district, or—where there are several Banks in the same locality—if all of these are in connection with each other, and form a system.

Where there is no central note-issuing Bank nor a connected system of banks, each bank will endeavour to prevent the notes of its rivals from circulating by presenting them for payment at the issuing Bank as soon as they come into its hands. The history of the first Chartered Banks in Scotland, the war between, and the subsequent reconciliation of the Bank of Scotland and the Royal Bank of Scotland, their joint action against any new competitors, and the final formation of a triumvirate, after the British Linen Company had been transformed into a Bank—all this affords a romantic illustration of the dangers and possibilities above referred to.

If the Charter of the Bank of Scotland had been renewed in 1716,[1] it is likely that a similar struggle to that witnessed in London would have ensued in Scotland. But apparently the Government wanted to provide posterity with an example of something more satisfactory.

The Scottish Banks opposed all endeavours

[1] This Charter was not renewed because the Bank of Scotland did not make any serious efforts to obtain its continuation when it lapsed, and when later, in 1727, it endeavoured to secure a renewal, the request was refused by the Government.

to rise in the banking world which were likely to cause them serious competition. Thus matters stood during the first half of the eighteenth century. As soon, however, as, through their efforts to establish branches, they were obliged to abandon their oligarchic attitude, increased competition not only induced them to offer greater facilities to the public, but also to extend their business and to make their credit available in more than one locality.[1]

The Bank of England was established in the midst of a rising banking community, which it was unable to repress, which it was obliged to recognise, and whose power in later years even outgrew its own. The only course left open to the Bank was, with the help of the Government, to prevent its rivals from ousting it from the position which it had attained. But it did not extend its business, nor did it offer credit facilities to the general public.

The Scottish Banks were obliged to do this so that they might earn a living. The Bank of England, on the contrary, was independent on account of its close connection with the State.

The regrettable results which such a con-

---

[1] *Cf.* Kerr, *History of Banking in Scotland.* In 1774 the endeavours of the Bank of Scotland to establish branches in the provinces were at last successful.

dition of affairs entailed south of the Tweed were thus not solely and entirely due to the banking monopoly. North of it the country has equally known bad bank management, crisis, and panic (*i.a.*, in 1772). There, however, co-operation existed between the different Banks, and their branches all over the country afterwards took care that assistance was easily obtainable. The support of the Bank of England was only available in London, and co-operation with this institution remained, until well into the nineteenth century, an illusion.

The business methods of the Bank of England may be compared with those adopted by private bankers. The time had not yet arrived when private initiative was to accomplish what the Bank of England had failed to do. The latter had entered the arena to fight any " private bankers " who might want to become its competitors. This struggle was decided in the Bank's favour, but the result was that each party followed an independent course, while leaving the other's sphere free.

The Bank of England became a note-issuing bank *par excellence*. Even towards the end of the eighteenth century we find that its deposits hardly exceeded £1,000,000 to £1,500,000, against a note issue amounting to £9,500,000.[1]

[1] 1797. The weekly returns which from the commencement

The finances of the country had been taken entirely out of the hands of the King. They had become public business. The Exchequer and the King's Private Purse parted company for good, and whilst the Bank of England remained the banker of the Government, the Royal Family had their own houses for this class of business (such as David Barclay, of Barclay, Bevan & Co., Drummond & Co., Coutts & Co.). The Bank's notes, on the contrary, were readily accepted by the public, and the only obstacle to an extensive circulation was the high denomination at which they were issued (£20).

The main business of the " private bankers " remained the receipt of deposits. It is true their notes continued to circulate side by side with those of the Bank of England, and even increased considerably in their total amount, but these notes never lost the character of deposit receipts. Their amount remained to be filled in at the time of issue, and in consequence varied according to the various transactions for which they were issued.[1]

This may require some further explanation. The " promissory notes " of the Gold-

of the year 1698 had been regularly entered in a book, have, at least as far as this early period is concerned, not been preserved amongst the records of the Bank.

[1] After 1729 Child & Co. used printed forms for their notes, but on these the amount was left blank.

smiths, now " private bankers," did not intrinsically differ from those of the Bank of
England ; but whilst the Bank endeavoured
to obtain capital by the issue of notes, that
operation remained a secondary one for the
" private bankers." On the other hand, the
deposit system very soon lost its attractions
for the Bank of England, but continued to
form the basis of the business of private
banking institutions.

In the autumn of 1696 the Bank announced
for the first time that it would no longer
allow interest on its " Running Cash Notes "
(deposits). It subsequently revoked this decision, but definitely ceased to allow interest
at the beginning of 1699.

The payment of interest on " Bank Bills "
was not discontinued until the eighteenth
century, but the exact date is not ascertained.[1]

Private bankers did not cease to allow
interest on deposits[2] until the latter half of the

[1] In 1706 the Bank again issued " Sealed Bills," " the better
to enable them to perform their contracts with the Government,
bearing interest at 2d. per cent. per day or £3 per cent. per
annum."

[2] This refers, of course, to deposits in account current only ;
on deposits for long periods, interest has always been allowed.

" An anecdote is told by one of the customers of the Bank "
(Child & Co., Ye Marygold, Strand), " that rather more than
half a century ago " (i.e., 1830) " his grandfather, having a considerable sum of money, was anxious to meet with a London
banker to take charge of it. With that view he took a journey
to London and visited several bankers, whom he consulted as
to the terms upon which they would take his money. The

eighteenth or until the nineteenth century, when their promissory notes were no longer in circulation, or had been considerably reduced in number.

This might be considered as a point in favour of Bagehot's argument that a bank begins its endeavours to gain popularity and public confidence by issuing notes, and, once it has succeeded in achieving this object, may content itself with the development of its deposit system.

The " private bankers," however, were not obliged to set to work in that manner. They took over the business as it existed, from the Goldsmiths, and these, as we have seen, were entirely dependent upon the funds which they received on deposit.

Still more remarkable is the way in which

bankers being anxious to accommodate him, one said he would allow him 2 per cent., another said 3 per cent., while a third hesitated as to what he would do. At last he went to Child's, where he stated his business and asked what interest they would allow upon so large a sum of money. The reply was, 'We shall be happy to take charge of your money, but we will not give you any interest for it.' This answer appeared so to gratify the old gentleman, that he exclaimed, 'Then this is the place for me!' And hereupon opened his account. His descendants still bank with the firm ; but Messrs. Child & Co. have given up their old practice of not allowing interest for money on deposit" (Hilton Price, *London Bankers*, p. 36, 1890 edition).

In the previous 8vo 1876 edition it is stated, "Have never swerved from their old practice of not allowing interest for money on deposit."

The change was evidently made between 1876 and 1890.

the Bank of England contrived to secure a footing. From the outset its opposition was exclusively directed against those who endeavoured to compete by issuing notes.[1]

Against these it invoked the protection of the Government. All other bankers it allowed to rise and fall as they pleased. Their notes, however, were not permitted to remain in circulation. As soon as any of them came into the Bank's grasp they were presented for payment, and a number of administrative regulations were made to provide for their immediate presentation and collection. The Goldsmith bankers on their side retaliated as a matter of course.

That the Bank itself gradually abandoned the deposit system is more clearly revealed by each successive Bank Act, of 1697, 1708, and 1742, in which the note issue was the main object which it endeavoured to secure. In addition, the Bank discontinued in 1694 the custom of discounting or granting loans to those only " who kept their cash with the Bank." As a precautionary measure it was provided that the officials entrusted with this task should know the last endorser and the

---

[1] *E.g.*, the struggle carried on in 1697 against the " Land Bank " and in 1700 against the " Sword Blade Company," which endeavoured to " undercut " the Bank by demanding only 4 per cent. on loans, and again in 1707 against the " Mine Adventurers of England," who had begun to issue an unlimited number of notes.

drawee " as persons of good repute and standing."

On the other hand, the cheque system had been developed with " private bankers " for close upon a century before the Bank of England decided to adopt it.

From the foregoing the following conclusions may reasonably be drawn.

The private bankers continued the business previously carried on by the Goldsmiths, who, acting chiefly as cashiers on behalf of their customers, based their business on the deposit system. Their promissory notes were issued solely to customers.

Subsequently the Bank of England entered the field. The Bank took over the business methods of the Goldsmiths, but in addition carried into practical execution an idea which had been suggested nearly half a century before, viz., of obtaining capital by means of issuing promissory notes.[1]

The Bank soon recognised that this was the most remunerative way of obtaining capital, and used its utmost endeavours to

[1] One of the best pamphlets dealing with this subject is that entitled *The Key of Wealth, or a New Way for Improving Trade*, by William Potter, published in London in 1650. In clearness it leaves nothing to be desired, but its length and its somewhat too elaborate form act as deterrents to intending students. *The Tradesman's Jewel or a safe easie speedy and effectual means for the incredible advancement of Trade*, published in the same year, suffers from the opposite defect.

prevent competition in this direction. In these efforts it was readily supported by the Government, who turned the Bank's issue of notes to their own advantage.

The " private bankers " were, as a matter of course, excluded from competition with the Bank in this branch, in view of the amount of capital with which the Bank of England carried on its operations and which was exceptionally large for those days. The efforts of the Bank of England were in consequence confined to opposing the competition of such limited companies as might be established —a competition which became especially acute between the years 1710 and 1720.

A note circulation which, within a quarter of a century, rose to about £5,000,000, exclusive of the Exchequer Bills in circulation, proved too much for the private institutions, the more so as this circulation was chiefly restricted to London and its immediate neighbourhood.[1]

[1] For the first year of its existence the turnover of the Bank of England amounted to £2,500,000. The highest amount of notes ever issued, *e.g.*, by Martin's Bank, remained within comparatively narrow limits.

" The amount owing on these notes was relatively small, and from the year 1750 to 1800 the total liability in this respect exceeded £10,000 only on thirteen occasions, an exceptional maximum being on one occasion reached in a total of £31,000."

The recognition of liability for note issue, as a matter of account, entirely ceased with Messrs. Martin in 1807. *Cf. The Grasshopper*, p. 136.

Even if the activity of the private bankers had not from the outset been confined to the deposit system, subsequent events would have gradually forced them to adopt the course in which they were now compelled to persevere.

Consequently the note circulation of the private bankers remained restricted to their customers, and the main object of these notes continued to be to facilitate the transfer of the capital entrusted to the bankers. Hence the customers by degrees ceased to use these notes and employed cheques, which were far better adapted to their purpose.[1]

These considerations enable us to understand clearly the relations between the Bank of England and the private bankers during the eighteenth century—a relationship which formed the basis for the development of the London banking system during the nineteenth century.[2]

[1] Whilst the first printed notes (Child & Co.) appeared in 1729, Martin's Bank were the first to issue printed cheques, between 1749 and 1759. Child & Co. followed their example in 1762. The last private bank-notes in London—those of Coutts & Co.—dated from the year 1843.

[2] A curious illustration of the less friendly feelings entertained towards the Bank of England is afforded by the fact that in 1707 Mr. Francis Child and Sir Richard Hoare accumulated a considerable number of notes of the Bank and presented the same simultaneously for payment. *Cf. Macleod*, i., p. 486. The historian Francis relates how a similar procedure was followed by the Bank of England towards Child & Co. in 1745, which however, in view of the above-mentioned dates (see Note on

In the course of the year 1697 the Bank of England was compelled to suspend payment of its notes. It was the first object-lesson to the Bank, that it is essential to keep a certain proportion of present capital in reserve, when the exchange of future against future capital only makes up a part of the ordinary business operations and when the receiving and supplying of present capital still represents a considerable item of that business. The lesson struck home, though, according to the opinions of the most competent critics, not by any means forcibly enough. It may be said that the Bank reserve dates from that period. The Bank's own notes were at that time presented for payment, whilst as a result of the conditions then prevailing the cash in hand had been reduced to a minimum.[1]

The Goldsmith bankers must previously have gained this experience, although apparently many of them only half realised the importance thereof. A number of them finally disappeared from the scene during these times,

previous page), seems hardly probable. No confirmatory evidence of such action has been discovered by Hilton Price in the books of his firm.

[1] The return submitted by the Bank to the House of Commons in December, 1696, clearly reveals the small cash balance available (£35,664 1s. 10d.) as against liabilities aggregating £2,101,187 13s. 5d., viz., about 1·7 per cent. (see, *i.a.*, Lawson's *History*, p. 74).

after having been obliged definitely to suspend payments.[1]

Ever since the question has remained a matter of controversy. Men of practical experience—that is to say, the bankers themselves—seldom adhere to maximum and minimum, or percentage, and if they do, only approximately. Bankers, however, as a rule write or publish very little. Hence Martin's maxims, a set of rules framed by Sir Thomas Martin, are the more remarkable.[2]

[1] *Cf.* Hilton Price, *London Bankers*, seriatim.

[2] *Cf. The Grasshopper*, p. 46.

The document is dated 1746, but its contents are of an earlier date. Sir Thomas Martin became a partner in the firm in 1703 and died in 1765. The rules have been written by Mr. E. Blackwell, who was admitted into partnership about 1746. It is not improbable that at the same time he adopted the principles of his senior partner, which were the outcome of long years of experience. Their peculiar interest is an excuse for reproducing the rules in their entirety :

"Proper Considerations for Persons Concerned in the Banking Business.

1. Some Judgment ought to be made of what sum is proper to be out at a constant interest.

2. A proportion of Bonds, Land tax tallies, and silver to be ready on a sudden demand.

3. A proportion of Government Securities, as Navy Bills.

4. Not to lend any money without application from the borrower and upon alienable security that may be easily disposed of, and a probability of punctual payment without being reckoned hard by the borrower.

5. All loans to be repaid when due, and ye rotation not exceed six months.

6. Not to boast of great surplus or plenty of money.

7. When loans do not offer, to lend on Stocks or other Securities, buy for ready money and sell for time.

Every banker will admit that at the present time these maxims may still be regarded as the primary requisites for sound bank management. They exhale prudence, but contain no hard and fast rule. The essential in the eyes of their framer was that the working capital should continue to circulate, but not remain outstanding for too long a period ; that a portion of the capital should be invested in readily realisable securities and another portion be retained in cash. Further, that in case of an unusual abundance of available funds the banker should place amounts for which no immediate demand was anticipated, with the Goldsmiths, *i.e.*, at short notice. Thus originated the present loans " at call."

At the same time it seems to appear from

8. When credit increases by accident upon an uncertain circulation the money may be lent to Goldsmiths, or discount bills of exchange.

9. 'Tis prudence and advantage of a Goldsmith that depend upon credit, to endeavour as near as possible upon the yearly settling Accounts to have the investure of that money in Effects that are easy to be converted into money.

10. To appear cautious and timorous contributes very much to give persons in credit an esteem among mankind.

11. Avoid unprofitable business, especially wn-attended with trouble and expense.

12. 'Tis certainly better to employ a little money at a good advantage, if lent safely, in order to have a greater cash by you, tho' possibly you may extend your credit safely.

13. When it shall be thought proper to call in old loans the demanding of them ought to be in the names of all the Partners."

9

these maxims that the practice of discounting bills did not originate with the bankers.

The most salient feature during this period is the tightening of the bonds between the Government and the Bank of England. Both made use of the financial needs of the State. The Bank was ready to listen to the demands of the Treasury, but with each loan it contrived to obtain authority to increase its share capital, thus extending the limits of its note issue. It is characteristic that the renewal of the Charter always took place years before its expiration.[1]

It is obvious that in these transactions the Government became more and more the moving spirit. Originally it was the Bank which was actuated by the desire to secure a monopoly, but subsequently the extension of the Bank Charter was the bait used by the Government to enlist the Bank's support for its financial proposals. The lion's share of the profits fell to the Bank. The Government generally under-estimated its own influ-

---

[1] The original Charter had been granted for twelve years. In 1697 it was renewed until 1710. In 1708 a further extension was granted to 1732. The Bank advanced a sum of £400,000 to the Government, free of interest, and took over Exchequer Bills (which did carry interest) to the amount of £1,700,000. For this purpose a fresh issue was made in 1709, by which the capital of the Bank was raised to £5,058,547. In 1713 the term was extended by ten years until August, 1742, and in consideration thereof the Bank undertook to issue £1,200,000 Exchequer Bills on behalf of the Government.

ence, whilst the Bank took full advantage of
the penurious condition of the Treasury.[1]

During the first thirty years of the Bank's
existence the debt of the Treasury to the
Bank grew in this way to £9,100,000 (that is
to say, about two-thirds of the entire Consolidated Debt which was incurred to the Bank
up to 1833) and in consideration hereof the
Charter was extended six times.

For the Treasury this method of obtaining
capital was wholly inadequate. The total
Government Debt during the same period increased to £30,000,000. If it had not been
for the clause inserted in the Bank Act of
1694, the Bank of England would probably
have taken over the entire Public Debt. As
matters stood now, its lending operations to
the Government were conducted on the same
lines as those of the Goldsmiths in former
times. The Bank anticipated the payment of
the taxes and enabled the Government to dis-

[1] *Cf.* Act 7 Anne, c. 7 (1708). Several clauses commence
thus : "And for the encouragement of the said Governor and
Company of the Bank of England" either "to advance and pay
the said sum of four hundred thousand pounds," or "to perform
the other services in this Act mentioned," or "to undertake
the circulation of the said (Exchequer) Bills," then follow the
clauses authorising "the said Governor and Company of the
Bank of England to increase their capital" by the amount
named in the Act and stipulating that the Bank "so enlarged as
aforesaid and their successors for ever shall remain, continue,
and be one body corporate and politick by the name aforesaid,"
and that it shall continue to enjoy the privileges bestowed upon
it or receive new ones.

pose at once of the probable proceeds, whilst the taxes came in gradually and were frequently not collected until years afterwards.[1] In reality, the Bank here again exchanged " short " for " long future capital."

Meanwhile serious endeavours were made, as early as the beginning of the eighteenth century, to consolidate the floating debt. Soon after 1711 a scheme was formulated and car-

[1] *Cf.* the Bank return published in 1797, to be found, *inter alia*, in Lawson, pp. 95–96, " an account of the amount of money advanced for the Public service by the Bank of England, and outstanding on the 25th February, 1797."

				£		
On Land Tax	...	1794	141,000			
" " ...	...	1795	312,000			
" " ...	...	1796	1,624,000			
" " ...	...	1797	2,000,000			
				4,077,000	0	0
Malt	...	1794	196,000			
"	...	1795	158,000			
"	...	1796	750,000			
"	...	1797	750,000			
				1,854,000	0	0
Consolidated fund ...	1796	1,323,000				
Vote of credit for £2,500,000	...	1796	821,400			
				2,144,440	0	0
				8,075,400	0	0
Exchequer Bills without interest	...		376,739	0	9	
				8,452,139	0	9
Treasury Bills of Exchange ..	...		1,512,274	2	3	
				£9,964,413	3	0

Cf. p. 177 *note.*

ried through by the then Chancellor of the Exchequer (Mr. Harley). A few merchants, to be incorporated into a Company, were to take over £9,500,000 of floating debt at 6 per cent. interest on condition that they should be granted the exclusive privilege of free commercial intercourse with the countries in the South Sea for a period of thirty-two years. This was the origin of the South Sea Company.

In spite of the opposition of the Bank of England, it was followed in 1717 by a second scheme of similar purport, again in favour of the same Company. The South Sea Company, which had been founded under the auspices of the Tory party, and of which the King was the President, was far more influential than the Bank of England, though it was not allowed to carry on banking business.

In 1720 the third and most notorious proposal was made, viz., to take over and liquidate the entire Public Debt. This operation was likewise granted to and undertaken by the South Sea Company ; with what result is sufficiently known.

The Bank of England in 1721 took over the liabilities left by its rival, whilst it was at the same time authorised to increase its own capital by an amount equal to the total sum of those liabilities.

Since that time the Government has never

again invoked the assistance of merchants in the amortisation of the Public Debt. The administration of the Debt remained in the hands of the Government officials. In increasing degrees the services of the Bank of England as banker to the Government were made use of, until at the present time this institution is indissolubly connected with the financial administration of the country.[1]

The struggle between the two above-named powerful financial institutions was the primary cause of this development. When, in 1717, the South Sea Company once again secured a victory over its adversary (though both had to content themselves with a substantial reduction in the rate of interest), the Bank of England obtained, by way of compensation, the privilege that all transfers of Public Debt and Public Stocks should be made in the Bank's books, and that the payment of interest should likewise be made at its offices. The Bank undertook these services gratuitously, on condition that its capital as well as its notes were to be exempt from taxation.

In the succeeding year (1718) the Bank of England for the first time received subscriptions for loans on behalf of the Government. This practice has never since been departed from. The Government recognised its con-

[1] For the history of this development cf. *Die Bank von ngland*, by Professor Philippovich von Philippsberg.

venience, and the Bank of England continued to be their agents for all similar transactions.

Amongst these transactions there is one, viz., " Bank circulation," which deserves closer examination, as it affords an illustration of the way in which the Bank, although maintaining a small reserve only for its current business, contrived to create an extra reserve against extraordinary liabilities.

The Bank of England had undertaken to issue Exchequer Bills on behalf of the Government. It carried this operation through by at once handing the entire sum to the Government as it was accustomed to do. Generally it amounted to £1,000,000 per annum, whilst the Bills had three, six, or twelve months to run. The Bills were then put into circulation by the Bank in the usual way.

In order to obviate the necessity of maintaining a special reserve against these bills in circulation, the Bank simultaneously offered for public subscription what was subsequently termed " Bank circulation " to an amount equal to the sum lent to the Government.

Every subscriber undertook to pay in cash 10 per cent. of the amount subscribed for, whilst he continued to be liable for the remaining 90 per cent. This remainder could be called up at any time, at the discretion of the Bank, but this measure hardly ever proved to be necessary, and was only rarely resorted

to. At the expiration of one year the sub-
scriber obtained repayment of the amount
called up in full. If he failed to comply with
any demands of the Bank for the payment of
further instalments, the 10 per cent. originally
paid was forfeited.

Interest was allowed on the following basis :

The amount of 10 per cent., paid up, carried
interest at 4 per cent.

Over and above this $\frac{1}{4}$ per cent. was paid
on the entire amount of the subscription.

If further calls were made, the rate of interest on the sums so paid was raised to 5
per cent.

Consequently, if no further payments beyond the 10 per cent. had been called for, the
Bank allowed $6\frac{1}{2}$ per cent. on the capital which
it·received.

On the other hand, the Bank received from
the Government interest at the rate of 3 per
cent. per annum on the total amount of the
Exchequer Bills, viz., on £1,000,000 or
£30,000. Its profits on such transactions
under ordinary circumstances consequently
amounted to £23,500.[1]

---

[1] The Bank received from the Government on
  £1,000,000 30,000
  Less 4 per cent. interest on £100,000 and $\frac{1}{4}$ per
  cent. interest on £1,000,000 6,500

  Balance £23,500

This method was first put into practice at an early date ; in any case it was followed long before 1739.[1]

In the books of Martin's Bank this account ceased to exist in 1760.

In 1750, " Bank circulation "—according to Francis—was also applied to the conversion of the Government Debt. The Bank provided in this way money for the conversion of the Public Debt whenever demands for its repayment were made. An initial payment to the Government was in such cases not required.[2]

Thus at an early date the Bank of England

[1] The oldest records of *The Grasshopper* still extant, dating from the year 1739, contain frequent references to Bank Circulation.

[2] *Cf.*, for further particulars regarding "Bank Circulation," the pamphlet already referred to, written in 1797 : *The History of the Bank of England.*

Martin, in *The Grasshopper* (p. 138, *et seq.*), does not give a very clear interpretation of this method of creating a reserve adopted by the Bank. Probably the pamphlet in question was not known to him. From the books of his bank it appears that on each instalment a premium of 2 per cent. or more was allowed, whilst evidence is also available that the calling up of further instalments was not an unusual occurrence.

" Circulation Notes for the call on £20 per cent. and for such part of the remaining £70 as was voluntarily paid into the 35th subscription—the subscription was for £1,200,000." If "35th" refers to the subscriptions for Bank circulation, and if, as stated by the author of the above-mentioned pamphlet, such subscriptions only took place once a year, this method must have originated during the early years of the eighteenth century. The books of the Bank of England, prior to the year 1700, do not reveal the existence of any such system.

introduced in more than one respect a system of business which—by distributing liabilites over a large number of persons—lessened the liabilities of the Bank. The Bank, whilst able to continue to supply capital in the usual manner, obtained at the same time the utmost security that the liabilities which it had incurred should be met.

CHAPTER III

1742–1826.—THE DEVELOPMENT OF THE SYSTEM OF THE LONDON MONEY MARKET AND THE REPEAL OF THE MONOPOLY OF THE BANK OF ENGLAND

PART I

A DECISIVE victory generally forms the basis of a new struggle. Unfortunately, the victor as a rule is not mindful of this fact, and abandons himself to the apparent calm which succeeds the raging storm.

The peculiar character of this third period is the relative pause in the progress of the Bank of England, and the simultaneous development around it of institutions which gradually cultivated the ground left fallow by the Bank. For fifty years the Bank enjoyed the undisputed possession of a monopoly; but, whilst at the commencement of this period the Bank did not hesitate to dictate to the Government and to make its attitude towards the Government conditional upon the latter's compliance with its demands, it had, towards the end of

the eighteenth century, become a mere tool
in the hands of the Government ; powerless,
because he who then held the reins of government concerned himself little about *privilegia
et mores* where the preservation of the independence of his country was at stake, and
where he conceived it his mission to show his
country the way that leads to supremacy.

With the exception of some changes in its
administration, the Bank of England remained as it was in 1742. Its deposits did
not increase to any appreciable extent. Its
note issue gradually expanded ; but, until the
suspension of specie payments in 1797, practically exclusively in the Metropolis and its
immediate vicinity, and although occasionally
banknotes found their way to the North
of England and were readily accepted by
the public, it was in the interest of the
rising country banks to prevent the Bank
of England notes from obtaining currency
outside London, as the notes might interfere
with the circulation of their own notes.[1]

[1] As we have previously stated, the large denomination of
these notes favoured these endeavours on the part of the country
banks. Their use of the Bank of England's notes consequently
was mainly restricted to the cases where large transfers of cash
had to be made, and then they remained in the tills of the
country banks and merchant   In order to facilitate such
remittances, the Bank in 1738 introduced "Bank Post Bills"—
that is to say, notes made payable at seven days' sight, "that in
case the mail was robbed the parties might have time 'to stop

It was not until 1759 that the Bank altered the denomination of its notes, introducing notes for £15 and £10. In 1794 the first £5 notes made their appearance, in 1797 those for £2 and £1. The latter issues, however, were not long maintained. They afforded an easy opportunity for forgery. Although by the Acts of 1697, 1729, 1734, and 1737 the penalty of capital punishment was attached to the forging of banknotes, yet the offence continued to be a general one.[1]

The idea that the act of forging banknotes constituted a grave offence was never fully realised by the multitude. The severest penalties proved ineffective. The disproportion which, according to public opinion, existed between crime and punishment excited sympathy with the unfortunate victims. The consequence was that the notes, which were most commonly forged, became unpopular themselves. A score of years afterwards their

payment of the bills ' (*cf.* Gilbart, i., pp. 41 and 138). In 1759 Bank Post Bills were also issued in denominations of £15 and £10.

[1] 8 and 9 William III. c. 20, par. 36 ; 2 Geo. II. c. 25 ; and 7 Geo. II. c. 32. The latter two referred to bills and the forging of banknotes, &c. Though originally temporary measures, they were subsequently confirmed by 9 Geo. II. c. 18, par. 1. The offence was qualified as felony. " Felony" was liable to capital punishment (*cf.* for the history Maberly Phillips, p. 79, *sqq.*). The offence continued to be classified as "felony," but the punishment was mitigated in 1820 by 1 Geo. IV c. 92, and altered into transportation for fourteen years.

issue was discontinued. With one single exception, in 1825, they were never reissued.
About 1820 capital punishment for the offence
of forging banknotes was abolished, followed
later by the abolition of this penalty " for
all crimes classified as forgery."

For fifty years after 1713 the Charter had
not been extended previously to the year of
its expiration. Both in 1742 and in 1764 its
renewal had taken place in the year in which
it would have expired. There were good
reasons for this regularity. After 1717 the
Government was able to obtain funds from
the Bank in other ways than by borrowing in
large sums.[1]

In 1764 the Charter had been prolonged
until August, 1786. But as early as 1781
a fresh extension was granted until 1812,
and in consideration thereof the Government
received £2,000,000 for three years at 3 per
cent. interest.

On one other occasion the date of expiration was not awaited. There was a similar
reason for this. In 1797 the Bank Restric-

[1] Gilbart, i., 36 : "1718. Subscriptions for Government
loans were first received at the Bank. From this period the
Government have found it the more convenient to employ the
Bank as their agents in all operations of this nature, than to
transact them at the Treasury or the Exchequer. The Bank,
becoming by degrees more closely connected with the Government, began to make advances of money in anticipation of the
land and malt taxes, and upon Exchequer bills and other
securities." *Cf.* p. 134.

tion Act had been passed, by which the notes
of the Bank of England were declared inconvertible. This Act immediately led to a pro-
test against the Bank monopoly ; an unsuccessful effort was made to obtain legal
sanction for the establishment of a new Bank.
When, in 1799, public opinion expressed
itself strongly in favour of such action, the
Bank of England succeeded in securing in
that year the renewal of its Charter for a
period of twenty-one years as from its date
of expiration in 1812, viz., until August, 1833,
by making an advance to the Government of
£3,000,000 for the term of six years free
of interest.

It was the last occasion on which the
Charter was renewed before the year of its
expiration. Previous to 1833 the Bank had
lost its monopoly.

The transactions of the Bank with the
Government represent the natural outcome of
the conditions prevailing at that time. The
advances made by the Bank in anticipation
and on the security of the taxes and the
Treasury bills did not suffice for the needs
of the Government. The taxes needed the
sanction of Parliament, and the Government
required more funds than Parliament would
grant it. At this juncture was passed the
notorious Act of William Pitt (20 Geo. III.
c. 32), by which the Bank was authorised to

discount bills for the Government to an unlimited amount.[1]

Thus, evasion of the real object of the
restricting clause in the Bank Charter of 1694
was rendered possible.

In all these dealings the Government is
the predominant partner. There is no longer
any question of new privileges. The only
compensation which the Bank received in consideration of its services was the renewal of
its Charter. Whilst originally the sum to be
advanced by the Bank was made the subject
of negotiations,[2] it is this time simply pre-

[1] 1793. "Declaring that the Bank should not be subject to
any penalties for advancing money to the Government for the
payment of bills of exchange, accepted by the Commissioners
of His Majesty's treasury, and made payable at the Bank.
The amount of the sums so advanced was required to be
annually laid before Parliament" (Gilbart, i., 44, 45). This was,
in fact, an act of indemnity for advances already made, but was
expressed in general terms.

[2] In this connection we may refer, *i.a.*, to a pamphlet dating
from the year 1742, entitled *An Appeal to the People of
England, the Publick Companies and Monied Interest, on the
Renewal of the Charter of the Bank*, p. 9. "A general Court
was held in 1742." The Governor "acquainted them" (the
proprietors) "that the Court of Directors *had been given to
understand*, that the sum propos'd to be lent, would not be
accepted ; and that the Persons who might be suppos'd to bring
the matter into the House of Commons, had refus'd to act in it,
unless some further monies were advanced." £1,200,000, with
interest, had first been offered ; £1,000,000, without interest,
finally agreed upon.

In the opinion of the author of this pamphlet this latter sum
was still too small in view of the fact that whilst interest on the
original debt had been reduced to 6 per cent., the Bank could

scribed by the Government. Pitt even succeeds in persuading the directors to comply with his financial demands against their own will.

Whilst in the Metropolis the struggle in the banking world had come to a standstill, the provinces began to assert themselves, and their demands were recognised and satisfied.[1] On the one hand, in so far as attempts made to satisfy these demands originated in the country itself independent banks came into being in the country districts in the same way as in London the Goldsmiths

still earn 3 per cent. on its entire capital, " which sums, I believe, no Persons, who know anything of the State of our Funds, would pretend to be made three and a half per Cent. for anywhere."

With regard to the shareholders' meetings the author informs us, on p. 8, that "we have not heard of any others call'd till this very lately, just upon the time of the expiration of their Charter."

The law of 1694 compelled the Bank to hold half-yearly meetings. A little farther on the author adds : "When General Courts were summoned, tho' only at the times appointed by the Charter."

The attendance of shareholders at such meetings was small and frequently they were not present at all, so that the Directors were on several occasions obliged to call such clerks as were shareholders from their work in order to make up the required quorum.

[1] The most reliable sources upon which the text is based in connection with this matter are Macleod's *Theory and Practice of Banking* ; Maberly Phillips, *Banks, Bankers and Banking in Northumberland*, &c. ; Hilton Price, *London Bankers* ; Gilbart, *History, Principles, and Practice of Banking* ; and Thornton, *On Paper Credit.*

had gradually developed into bankers. The safe-keeping of cash offered the same difficulties in the country as in former times it had done in London, but the dangers attending the dispatch of money to and from the capital were still more serious. Contemporary accounts abound with tales of the holding up and robbing of coaches and other means of conveyance. They may be compared to the narratives of travellers in the solitary regions of North America in the eighteenth century. If the coaches were unreliable, this qualification applied in a still more pronounced degree to their drivers.[1]

It is probable that the country merchants, having business relations in London, after some unpleasant experiences, were not long in recognising that to them it was as great a convenience to keep an account current with a London banker as to the persons residing in London itself. When once this custom was adopted, and had met with general favour, the inference that merchants were frequently requested by friends to render them service by means of their account current seems a natural one. Gradually, when these requests multiplied to such an extent as to make it more profitable for the merchant to change

---

[1] It was no rare event for the coachman to conspire with the highwaymen or, in default of the latter, himself to act in a double capacity.

his account current in London in his own name as a private person to an account in his name as a banker, the friendly service had been transformed into a business transaction, and, when circumstances allowed, banking became to the merchant a separate business.

The deposit of cash with third parties was a branch which did not develop so quickly. Hoarding remained a common practice in the country.[1]

There were persons, however, to whom in the regular course of their business large sums of money were entrusted. The tax collectors, *e.g.*, were paid in specie. On account of the dangers attendant upon the transmission of money they were authorised to retain the funds under their care until an opportunity presented itself for remitting the amount in a bill to London.[2]

---

[1] The guilds kept their cash in large boxes called " hutches." In the same way we find " town hutches." A curious instance of hoarding is found in the will of Richard Belassis, of Morton Grange, Houghton-le-Spring, published in Surtees Society's publications, vol. xxxviii. This fortune consisted of : "Old angles, old rials and new rials or sovereigns, English crowns, French crowns, shillings, testons, current coin of gold, double ducats, old nobles, &c. One sum of £400, made up of shillings and testons, was put edgeways into a box, walled up, in a hollow place, within the wall of the newe great chamber." A considerable portion of the money had been wrapped in paper or lead and hidden in the most out-of-the-way places. These spots themselves were described in the will (see Maberly Phillips, p. 21).

[2] According to an announcement in the *London Gazette* of

Those in possession of " strong-rooms," too, were equipped to undertake the safe custody of funds belonging to third parties. Thus it came about that merchants and manufacturers obliged their customers and friends by keeping their cash.

In the same way as elsewhere the simple transaction of the deposit was gradually converted by the depositories into a double one ; they began to employ the funds entrusted to them in their own business and to allow interest thereon.

As far as the rural districts were concerned, travelling merchants sometimes granted credit to, or accepted money on behalf of, their clients for the period elapsing between their spring and autumn visits. They charged and allowed interest on such funds.

Some country banks also owe their origin to the keen instinct of their founders, who assisted the travellers passing through their district by effecting payments, and thus came into contact with the London banking houses.[1]

July 9–13 1696, the remittance of bills was permitted in view of the small amount of coin in circulation (owing to the new coinage) in order not to drain the country entirely of coin.

[1] As an instance in point we may cite the first bank in Newcastle, founded by Ralph Carr in 1755. Carr rendered special services in the war against the Pretender in 1745, when the Duke of Cumberland marched his army through Newcastle and had to pay his troops in gold. Through this he came into relation with Coutts of Edinburgh (later of London) and with Mr. Campbell, of London.

Many others, probably the majority, have grown out of well-patronised shops.[1]

On the other hand, endeavours were made by London houses to establish connections in the country : not, however, by the Bank of England, which contented itself with the extension of its circulation due to the fact that its notes were frequently preferred to bullion for transmission outside London, but by the private bankers. London banking firms not only entered into relations with provincial merchants who visited London and who frequently established themselves as bankers in the country, but it also often happened, especially towards the end of the eighteenth century, that London banking firms delegated a junior partner to some provincial town, where the latter, after acquainting himself with local conditions, opened a banking business, in conjunction with the senior partners resident in the City.

Although these banks could not exactly be

[1] For instance, the Old Gloucester Bank sprang from the candle-shop of Mr. James Wood (see Martin's *Stories of Banks and Bankers*, p. 138, *sqq.*). Especially characteristic is the history recorded on p. 140, *et seq.*, of the large London firm of Smith, Payne, and Smith, which originated in a flourishing draper's shop in Nottingham. Martin gives 1716 as the year of the foundation of the Old Gloucester Bank, a date which it is difficult to verify. For further particulars regarding the development of country banks on these lines we refer to the account thereof given by Thornton in his work *On Paper Credit*, Chap. VII.

termed " branches," they constituted links in the chain of banking institutions by which England was to be encircled.

The method last described was certainly not the first to be employed. But whichever may have been the first, it is a fact that, during the years immediately following the establishment of the country bank at Stafford by Mr. Stevenson in 1737,[1] country banking did not increase to any marked degree, so that in 1750 there were but a dozen of such institutions established in England.[2]

The development of country banks does not assume large proportions until after the above-mentioned year. It coincides with the revolution brought about by the improvement in the means of transit and the inventions in the domains of industry. The economic changes which were occasioned thereby, especially in the North of England, were bound to entail an exceptional demand for capital. This was still further increased by the general extension of trade and commerce.

The large demand for capital induced many to meet the same in a generous manner. Credit was granted liberally, but not always wisely and on a sound basis. The number of country banks established by 1772 equalled the number already in existence in 1750.

[1] Or the Old Gloucester Bank in 1716.
[2] Cf. Macleod's Dictionary, voce "Banking."

At the end of the eighteenth century their ranks had swollen to four hundred.

A peculiar feature of all these banks was that from the outset they supplied future capital against future capital. Where money was borrowed from them they paid in notes. Whilst originally country banking was based on the deposit system, it did not gradually lead to the keeping of cash on behalf of the customers and the system of notes and cheques resulting therefrom, as in the case of the Goldsmiths.

The note circulation of the country banks owed its origin rather to the commercial and industrial development of England. Following the example of the Bank of England, the multitude of small bankers which during the last half of the eighteenth century had sprung up in the country secured capital by the issue of promissory notes. It seems incorrect to attribute their origin exclusively to the circumstances above referred to as is done by Macleod.[1] By far the majority sprang up in the North of England, and their history—as described by Maberly Phillips— gives us a somewhat different impression than do Macleod's general remarks on the subject of the country banks.[2]

[1] *Theory and Practice of Banking*, vol. i., pp. 506–7.
[2] Evidence of the difficulty frequently experienced by a deposit bank in placing the funds at its disposal in the district

Unquestionably there was much chaff amongst the corn. But it should not be forgotten that when banks began to be established in the country those in London and Scotland were already past the earlier stages of development. The banks founded later, especially in the North of England, were imitations of the institutions which, in the localities just referred to, had already attained a certain measure of prosperity ; and, although country banking showed itself in its most favourable aspect in the northern provinces, it must be conceded that to draw attention exclusively to the weak points of the system is taking a very one-sided view. Those whose operations were conducted on sound lines, and who were able to maintain their position, formed the very foundations on which the present banking system in England has been built up.[1]

Difficult times were in store for the country banks. The sudden prosperity and the pro-

which constituted its direct sphere of activity was afforded, *i.a.*, by the case of the Old Bank of Newcastle. In 1755 this bank was established. On April 18, 1758, the partners adopted the following resolution : "Whereas the sums advanced by us on notes and accepted bills are found insufficient to employ the cash in our hands, we have agreed that any sums of money not exceeding £7,000 be lent out " (Maberly Phillips, p. 179).

[1] A much more appreciative opinion on, and a more correct picture of the influence exercised by, the country banks than Macleod's is given by Thornton, *loc. cit.*

gress made in every direction led to speculation ; consequently the business undertaken
was frequently out of proportion to available
means, and the inevitable result was the crisis
of 1772, the first serious crisis in England
itself [1] after the big South Sea Bubble.

A still heavier blow was dealt by the crisis
of 1793, which was due to practically identical
causes.

The banks were not yet strong enough to
weather such crises. As soon as confidence
had been shaken by the failure of one single
firm a panic ensued, which began with a run
on the bankers, whose notes were presented
to them for payment in large numbers.

If the difficulties connected with the accumulation or the transmission from London
of a certain quantity of specie within a short
time are taken into consideration, some con-
ception may be gained of the consternation
which was thus created, especially in view of
the likelihood that one after another the banks
would be compelled to suspend payments.

These difficulties are commonly attributed
to the clause in the Bank of England Charter,
by which, according to the interpretation
generally placed upon the text of this clause,

[1] English houses had been involved in the Hamburg-
Amsterdam crisis of 1763, but this had only hit a particular
class of merchants and had been chiefly confined to London.
Now whole districts and members of all classes of the community were affected.

the establishment of large banking institutions was rendered impossible. The monopolistic position of the Bank of England, which institution did not itself endeavour to meet capital requirements throughout the country, should no doubt to a large extent be held responsible for this state of affairs.

On the other hand, it remains an open question whether larger institutions with bigger capital would or could have guarded against the faults now committed by the smaller banking firms. The deplorable condition of the coinage would not thereby have been improved, neither would the distances have been shortened, nor, probably, a larger reserve of cash have been held. For what amount of cash reserve, be it ever so large, is able to withstand a " run "? The last resource in such circumstances is the possibility of immediately converting the paper reserve into cash.[1]

[1] A striking example of this is provided by the run on the Birkbeck Bank in London in the late summer of 1892. This run was unjustified, as most runs are, but it was confined to this bank, and the Bank of England and the Union Bank were thus able to advance to it hundreds of thousands of pounds in gold on its Consols and other securities. The "run" caused the staff of the bank much annoyance, but not for a single moment was there any danger of its being unable to meet its liabilities.

It was a curious feature that some of the frightened customers withdrew their deposits at one counter only to pay them in again at another, satisfied with the knowledge that the money was actually available.

This was rendered impossible by the distance separating them from London. Mutual assistance was out of the question, every one being intent upon self-preservation only. Moreover, even the most implicit confidence is not proof against a panic. The events which occurred during the year 1745 demonstrate that a national calamity could shake public confidence even in the Bank of England.

Maberly Phillips relates how during the period from 1772 to 1882 the leading merchants and residents of Newcastle and York met on no less than six occasions,[1] and decided to accept the notes of the three banking institutions in the district in payment at any time. To this decision publicity was given. It was arrived at after the affairs of these banks had been carefully examined and found in order.

There is another point which throws light on the causes of the difficulties in which the

---

[1] In 1772, 1792-3, 1797-1803, 1815, and 1816. In 1745 the leading merchants in London at a meeting held at Garroway's Coffee House, on September 26th, took a similar decision in respect to the Bank of England : "We, the undersigned, merchants and others, being sensible how necessary the preservation of public credit is at this time, do hereby declare, that we will not refuse to receive bank notes in payment of any sum of money, to be paid to us, and we will use our utmost endeavours to make all our payments in the same manner." The resolution had been signed by 1,140 persons before 4 p.m. on the succeeding day.

banks were involved. The business itself was not at fault, nor was the temptation of exceeding the limits imposed by available means alone responsible. In this instance the effect of such temptation would have shown itself in an adequate cash reserve at the banks. In many cases it was the old story, the disregard of the sound adage which at the present day is still impressed upon those who are desirous of getting on in the world, " every man to his trade." The fever of speculation had spread to the bankers, and the misfortunes which befell them reacted on their customers.[1]

From the outset the country banks entertained business relations with banks in London. Transactions with their agents chiefly consisted in the transmission and receipts of specie.

For instance, landlords received their rents twice a year, in May and November. These sums were remitted to London in bills, if

[1] This is clearly expressed in an announcement in the *Newcastle Chronicle* of July 25, 1772 : " So great are the losses and inconveniences sustained by many individuals from a late bankruptcy, that a great number of eminent merchants and gentlemen of fortune at a meeting held for that purpose, have come to a resolution not to keep their cash at any bank, who jointly or separately by themselves or agents, are known to sport in the alley in what are called bulls or bears, since by one unlucky stroke in this illegal traffic, usually called speculations, hundreds of their creditors may be ruined ; a species of gaming that can no more be justified in persons so largely intrusted with the property of others, than that of gambling at the hazard tables."

obtainable. When bills were scarce and at times commanded so high a premium that the expensive carriage of bullion was, after all, the cheapest way of effecting such remittances, the expenses connected with the transmission of bullion outweighed the profits which the bank in other times had derived from these transactions.

Yet they continued regularly to attend to these transactions, in view of the fact that the tenants had been instructed by the landlords to accept the notes of the banks in payment for their corn.

The discounting of bills constituted the chief means by which, in industrial districts, the banks supplied capital. In agricultural districts, on the other hand, loans predominated. Where the population occupied itself partly with agriculture, partly with industry, both systems prevailed.

Before the history of the country banks is continued, some brief comments may be made on the history of the private banks in London. Whilst in the provinces the issue of notes gradually expanded and became more popular, the reverse was the case in London. Towards the end of the eighteenth century almost all private banks had discontinued the issue of notes. This was counterbalanced by the growing increase of the use of cheques.

In a previous chapter reference has already been made to the general reasons for this change. The surrounding circumstances supplied further reasons. The desire to connect stages of development with historical events accounts for the fact that the discontinuance of the private note circulation in London is generally ascribed to the crisis of 1772. It cannot be gainsaid that this crisis helped to give a final blow to the already tottering system. The collapse of several commercial and banking firms caused the notes of their neighbours to be likewise presented for payment. In many instances payment was refused—an occurrence detrimental to both parties. To those who had survived the crisis the danger which their note issue presented was forcibly brought home ; a danger which—without justification perhaps—is considered less grave, in the case of deposits, when an established *clientèle* [1] has

---

[1] As an illustration of the fact that an established *clientèle* does not necessarily impart confidence, and that mistrust frequently originates in the most insignificant circumstance, we may quote the following story, dating from the end of the eighteenth or the beginning of the nineteenth century :

"Old Mr. Fuller (Fuller, Banbury & Co.), of Cornhill, belonged to that very old-fashioned, prim class of bankers, well known in the last century, who were hardly ever absent from their desk in the shop and who slept always over the bank. He was a careful, economical man, who always had his washing done at home. One day every week, at noon, a pint of beer was brought in and placed at the foot of the stairs for the washerwoman, washing day being always known in the City by this circumstance. Once, however this pint became a pot. News

to be reckoned with. This was another reason why that branch of the business was abandoned.

The cheque system offered a serious objection of another kind, viz., the circumstance that payment had to be obtained from the banker named on the cheque. The Goldsmiths had already endeavoured to meet this inconvenience by keeping mutual accounts-current, thus enabling them to settle a large proportion of their reciprocal claims by transfers over their respective accounts.

This system, however, was never generally adopted ; it remained necessary that the different banks should send their clerks to present the demands which they held in the form of notes or cheques, at the respective offices whence they were issued, whenever circumstances required it, and to demand payment of the same. Frequently such payment was effected in cheques or notes drawn on, or issued by, the banker presenting the said demands for payment. Whenever necessary, the balance was settled in gold or notes

of the unheard of innovation quickly spread, and caused quite a sensation in Lombard Street and Cornhill. Indeed, an old customer called upon him to remonstrate upon his extravagance, telling him that, although he had had satisfaction in keeping his accounts with him till then, he now hardly considered him fit to take charge of other people's money, since he did not know how to take care of his own." (F. Hilton Price, *London Bankers*, p. 63.)

(either their own or those of the Bank of England).

For this purpose the bankers kept separate clearing books, which were in use with Child & Co. as early as 1753.[1]

Whilst therefore the banks followed a system of compensation whenever possible, the clerks on their part, being obliged to run backwards and forwards to the various offices, gradually saved each other the trouble of demanding payment at the offices of the respective bankers. The majority of them belonged to offices which were situated in Lombard Street, which caused the clerks to meet each other frequently. This led to interchange of information regarding the mutual demands on each others' houses, and the subsequent exchange of the documents which represented the respective demands. Soon these occasional encounters developed into daily meetings at a certain fixed place in order to save each other as much inconvenience as possible. At length the bankers themselves resolved to organise these meetings on a regular footing in a room specially reserved for this purpose.[2]

---

[1] Hilton Price, *London Bankers, voce* " Clearing House," p. 38. At the " Grasshopper " these books are still termed " Goldsmiths' Books."

[2] According to contemporary accounts these meetings were originally held in the open air at one of the banking houses which had a broad window-sill protruding into the street.

It is impossible to state with precision when the Clearing House was established, but very probably it was prior to 1773.[1]

As soon as the most serious objection to the use of cheques had been surmounted their use developed into a system. Towards the end of the eighteenth century " crossed cheques " began to be adopted in London.[2] Such cheques could, however, only become

The noise connected with this exchange became so obnoxious to those working inside the bank, that railings were constructed round the window-sill, a very efficient means of restoring quiet !

Since then—so the tale goes—the clearing has been carried on inside.

[1] In the books of the *Grasshopper* we find the following entry :

	s.	d.
1773 to quarterly charge for the use of Clearing Room	19	6

The establishment of the Clearing House is naturally connected with the extension of the cheque system ; and as regards the latter it should be remembered that Martin's Bank issued printed cheques between 1749 and 1759, Child's Bank in 1762. The clearing books of the latter institution point equally to the fact that the London clearing commenced at an earlier date than is generally understood. *Cf.* Martin, *Grasshopper*, pp. 167 and 168, where, *i.a.*, the list of members of the Clearing House for 1774 is given.

[2] Crossed cheques are such as can only be presented through a banker to the bank on whom they are drawn. This is indicated by writing on the cheque, between two parallel vertical lines drawn across the cheques, either the name of a specified banking firm or merely the words " & Co." In the first case the cheque is termed " specially crossed " in the latter " generally crossed."

useful, when the custom of keeping accounts with a banker had become a general practice.

Circumstances favoured the development of this custom. Undoubtedly the position of the Bank of England during the closing years of the eighteenth century and the suspension of its specie payments in 1797 is largely responsible for the extension of the business of the " private bankers."

When trade and industry began to recover from the crisis of 1772 the increased activity in this direction was accompanied by a rapid expansion of the note issue in the provinces.

The existing banks were the first to benefit by the movement. The country was in need of capital. As production had received a new stimulus and had entered a new period, the result of which would only show itself after a considerable time, it is obvious that all present capital was requisitioned, whilst its equivalent in future capital would only be available after a correspondingly remote period.

Under these conditions it need not cause surprise that deposits did not increase to any material extent, and that, on the other hand, a considerable expansion of the notes in circulation took place.[1]

[1] Maberly Phillips reproduces on p. 46 the following return of the Old Bank of Newcastle :

The longer the period of peace the greater the number of those who were induced by the example of others to devote themselves to banking. All banks which were established about this time were banks of issue. Especially after the crisis of 1783, during the period of five years from 1785 to 1790, a number of country banks started business. They freely discounted the bills offered to them, paid for them in their own notes, and thus largely increased the circulating medium of the country.[1]

In 1756 circulation £13,500, deposits £10,000, capital £2,000
In 1776   „   180,000   „   85,000   „   8,000
In 1777   „   128,000   „   37,000   „   8,000

He attributes the decline in the latter year to the number of new banks which had been established.

[1] The fact that the book-credit deposit system was not yet developed should not be lost sight of. In 1793, twenty-four out of a total of twenty-seven banks in Northumberland were banks of issue, and their aggregate issue was estimated at £680,000. The four banks in Newcastle alone accounted for £230,000, whilst the remaining twenty had an issue of about £450,000 (Maberly Phillips, p. 57).

Endeavours were made in 1788 to establish a Clearing House in Newcastle, without, however, any lasting results. We refer to this question in the text in a subsequent paragraph. A condition for the successful operation of the clearing system is a close understanding between a number of banks which have a sphere of activity extending over a fairly wide area. In Scotland conditions were more conducive to the success of the system. The branch banks which formed part of one central institution co-operated with each other as a matter of course, whilst they together covered a wider field than one single institution could have embraced. It seems also natural that the demands as between branches and head office

As already mentioned above, their number increased in 1793 to near four hundred.

The Bank of England now began to occupy a central position in the English banking system. The standard of the coinage in England had practically changed during the eighteenth century. Silver had become so scarce that, especially in the provinces, a decided dearth of small circulating medium made itself felt.

It was not long before the deficiency was met by the issue of paper money. Notes of three, five, and seven shillings were put into circulation in large numbers.[1]

The Government energetically opposed this latter measure. In 1775 notes below twenty shillings, and in 1777 those below £5, were prohibited. The banks were compelled to fall back upon gold as their cash reserve.

In the provinces no cash reserve, or, at any rate, no adequate cash reserve, was kept. The gold which in times of prosperity found its way to the banks and was not immediately

and between branches amongst themselves should be settled by a system of clearings.

[1] The *Scotch Magazine*, July 25, 1774: " Tickets of three-, five-, and seven-shilling pieces, payable at sight, the same as bank notes, are issued by a capital person of most towns in England, which pass current, and are a great relief at this time to tradesmen, especially when gold, particularly quarter-guineas, is so much scrupled by the farmers and country people."

required by them was at once forwarded to their London agent.[1]

To quote a single instance : the firm of Backhouse & Co., of Newcastle, remitted in one single year, from December, 1778, to November, 1779, 34,990 guineas to the Metropolis.[2]

The natural consequence was that in times of adversity the converse movement took place, and the bankers in the provinces drew gold from the capital.

In this respect their position differed from that of the Scotch banks. These latter formed a separate group, subject to special legislation. The English banks were all governed by one uniform law, and from the outset the country bankers became closely associated with the London banking system.

Although they kept a till for their daily requirements and special demands which might arise under ordinary circumstances, they were not prepared for emergencies. Apart from their deposits with the " private banks " in London, they had no command over a central cash reserve upon which they

[1] The gold transfers after 1772 probably contributed to the increase of the number of banks in the provinces. They should be looked upon as remittances. The provinces and London in those times may be looked upon, for all practical purposes, as two different countries.

[2] Maberly Phillips, p. 59.

could fall back in case of need. And if the bankers themselves did not possess any specie, it was hardly probable that it could be obtained anywhere else in their district. They were obliged to rely upon London.

On the other hand, it could hardly be expected that their London agents would keep a separate cash reserve for the country banks apart from their ordinary cash, which probably consisted partly of banknotes. If the country banks had insisted upon this, and had permanently kept a special deposit with the London bankers for this purpose, the matter would have been different. But this was not their policy. Their London agents were intermediaries, through whom payments were made and received.[1] In case of need the agents themselves fell back upon the Bank of England.

Here undoubtedly we are confronted with the weak side of the organisation of the country banks in the eighteenth century, viz., the inadequacy of the cash reserve maintained even by those banks which obtained a longer lease of life than that secured by the ephemeral creations of a boom.

The historic character of the English

---

[1] When the balance to the credit of a country bank had reached a considerable figure, it was generally invested. Thus Lambton & Co. (of Newcastle) instruct their agents on March 9, 1793, to buy consols to an amount of £10,000 "as they had a considerable balance at their London agents'."

money market is thus once more revealed. Its system of keeping one central reserve is an old-established institution and no invention of modern times.

The Bank of England was a powerful body with a large capital. Its extensive operations with the State and its note issue required the maintenance of an adequate cash reserve, or at least of one which exceeded the reserves kept by other bankers. The latter were able to meet demands in Bank of England notes, but the Bank was obliged to satisfy its own engagements in specie.

The Government used the Bank's services in order to improve the coinage by entrusting it with the withdrawal of old and worn-out coins while new coins were being minted, and with the issue of the latter as soon as they came from the Mint. On the one hand it received bad coins and on the other it had to effect all payments in unclipped, heavy coins.

As an ever-increasing number of private banks gradually abandoned the issue of notes, this condition of affairs became more and more the normal one. Concurrently therewith the Bank of England notes acquired greater prominence.

As time went on the public grew familiar with the changed circumstances and accepted them. On the Bank emerging unshaken from each successive crisis confidence in its notes increased, and they were readily accepted at any time.

It is to be regretted that the Bank directors did not sufficiently appreciate this fact, and as a result thereof aggravated matters, both for themselves and others, at the' critical moment.

The first crisis during which direct assistance was expected from the Bank of England by the other banks took place in 1783. The crises of 1762 and 1772 had been confined to the commercial world. The number of banks throughout the country was still relatively insignificant,[1] and they had not yet closely identified themselves with commercial interests.

While the first of these periods is generally regarded as the one marking an increase in the popularity enjoyed by the note issue of the Bank of England, the second may be considered as the period of the extension of its note issue over the whole' of England and Wales. This took place especially during the prosperous years immediately preceding 1783. Whilst in 1780 the value of the notes in circulation was about £6,500,000, this amount had risen to £9,500,000 in 1783.

[1] In 1776 the number of country banks was estimated at 150, in 1790 at 350. In London only 68 banks existed at the commencement of the nineteenth century.

About this time the Bank adopted the unfortunate theory that the note circulation should be contracted simultaneously with an efflux of gold from the Bank, in order to bring about a reflux of the specie withdrawn, owing to the scarcity of circulating medium created by this action. The author of this idea was Mr. Bosanquet.[1]

The number of notes in circulation can, however, only be reduced by refusing bank facilities. In December, 1782, the Bank of England began to discriminate in its discounting of bills and its loan operations. This attitude precipitated the crisis. Distrust began to spread; the bankers strengthened their cash reserves. Instead of an influx of gold from the provinces, a demand set in for the yellow metal from this very quarter. In May, 1783, the cash in hand at the Bank of England had fallen to £475,000. It refused further loans to the Government, whilst many merchants found it impossible to get their bills discounted.

Circumstances favoured the Bank. The foreign exchanges turned in favour of

[1] This theory should not be confused with the one which maintains that with a note issue the foreign exchanges should be especially watched. According to Mr. Bosanquet the single fact sufficed that gold was withdrawn from the Bank irrespective of the question whether it was required for internal circulation or for abroad. The theory, as amended, found its way into the Bank Act of 1844.

England, and the gold which came from abroad flowed into the vaults of the Bank and reinforced its cash reserves. The Bank was then able to apply the reverse of the above theory, viz., to issue banknotes freely, in proportion to the increase of its bullion, and the crisis thereby was overcome. In the meantime the number of failures had been legion.

The crisis of 1793 entailed more serious consequences. Trade had expanded, so to speak, by leaps and bounds. The improved means of transit, the opening up of numerous fresh markets after the conclusion of peace with America, and the commercial treaty with France in 1786 had each in their turn given an impetus to a fresh period of speculation, similar in character to that which followed the advent of the railways in the middle of the next century. The more abruptly such speculation was checked, the more violently the causes operated which necessitated a general liquidation and the graver became the crisis.

New banks had sprung up in hundreds, and their liabilities, as well as those of the existing institutions, had assumed considerable proportions. This time credit facilities had been extended chiefly to commerce, and the interests of the banks were closely connected with trade conditions. The note circulation had risen to nearly £10,000,000.[1] The note issue of the Bank of England had expanded from £6,000,000 (in 1784) to £12,000,000 (in 1793), whilst the amount of discounted bills which it held had risen during the period 1791-3 from £1,800,000 to £6,400,000.[2]

As the two preceding crises had not checked, but only temporarily retarded, the economic progress of the country,[3] the liabilities resulting from this huge note issue were to a large extent represented by new machinery, by improved means of communication in the interior, viz., by fixed capital.[4]

---

[1] This estimate is based on the note issue of the banks in Northumberland (cf. p. 162, note 1) and does not include the banks of Lancashire which did not issue notes.

[2] Cf. Clément Juglar, p. 299, et seq.

[3] This is partly illustrated by the expansion of trade during the period 1782–92 :

	Imports.	Exports.	Average Tonnage of Vessels.
1782	£10,300,000	£13,000,000	777
1792	£19,000,000	£24,900,000	1,871

Cf. Clément Juglar, loc. cit.

Especially if it be borne in mind that the inventions of Watt, Arkwright, and Brindley did not find general application throughout the kingdom until years after they had been given to the world.

[4] D. Macpherson, Annals of Commerce, p. 265, sqq. Of the "wealth accumulated in nine peaceful years of successful commerce, a very considerable proportion was invested in machinery and inland navigation."

When the crisis came, and after the first failures had produced a panic, in consequence of which no one could obtain assistance : " it was impossible to raise any money upon the

The declaration of war against France in 1793 precipitated the general reaction.

The crisis originated in London. As early as November, 1792, the number of failures had increased to an alarming extent. In March and April of the succeeding year the suspension of payments by commercial houses became general, and they carried the bankers with them in their fall. Many of these were " agents " of the banks in the country.

Their disappearance was naturally followed by the appointment of others in their place. This did not pass unnoticed. The public wrongly interpreted the fact ; it became frightened, and lost confidence in the country banks. In ever increasing number, their notes were presented to them for conversion into gold. As had happened in 1782, the banks had sufficient command of bullion to meet the growing demand ; and whilst in the

security of machinery or shares of canals ; for the value of such property seemed to be annihilated in the gloomy apprehension of the sinking state of the country, its commerce, and manufactures." This corresponds with the resolution of April 18, 1758 (see p. 151, note 2) to the effect that it was so difficult to find "genuine banking investment for funds." When, therefore, commerce revived during the nine years preceding 1793 it was only natural that the country banks should seize the opportunity and freely lend future capital (in the shape of short future capital) against future capital (in the shape of long future capital). In his *Dictionary*, *voce* " Crisis," Sir Inglis Palgrave ascribed the prevailing difficulties to "too heavy advances on insufficient or inconvertible securities and an over-stimulated spirit of mercantile enterprise."

provinces hundreds anxiously waited outside the bank offices for the moment when it would be their turn to enter, several of the partners, some of them accompanied by a number of their clerks, ran about in London, equally anxious to find a place where they could obtain gold for their securities. If they were fortunate enough to secure the cash, they hurried back in spite of all the dangers which awaited them on the journey.

It was of no avail. Not much time elapsed ere rumours came in from all sides that country banks, though completely solvent according to their books, had been compelled to suspend payment in default of cash.[1]

This time the Scotch banks shared their fate. In Glasgow especially conditions were critical. From Scotland also the bankers

---

[1] *Cf.* Maberly Phillips, *loc. cit.*, p. 48. Of the 400 country banks, 100 disappeared from the scene and the remaining 300 suspended payments. "The very bank that reported all *quiet and undisturbed*" (Lambton & Co.) on March 20th had, before the close of the month, first a clerk and then two partners in London seeking gold; a supply of which they obtained, and carried north with all speed. "In Newcastle things had grown desperate. From Monday, April 1st, to Saturday, the 6th, all the banks had been sorely pressed but stood their ground. Then the proprietors of the 'Commercial' felt that they could hold out no longer. On Monday, the 8th, they informed their friends that they had to stop payment for some time." And this notwithstanding a surplus of £25,000.

On that day and on the 10th following the merchants again resolved to accept nevertheless the notes of the banks in payment (*cf.* p. 155).

came to London with the same object as their English neighbours. This certainly did not allay the consternation.

The discounting of bills or the obtaining of loans in London was beset with the greatest difficulties. The Bank of England had, in December, 1792, begun to carry out the policy previously referred to.[1]

Whilst throughout the country specie became scarce, in addition a shortage of a fiduciary circulating medium, which enjoyed full confidence on the part of the public, began to be felt.

The situation became untenable. Sir John Sinclair, M.P.,[2] succeeded in convincing the Government that intervention was essential to save the country from greater calamities.

As the Bank of England withheld its support, the State assumed the duty of providing assistance, and, as it had done on a previous occasion—a century earlier—it placed fiduciary circulating medium at the disposal of the banking community.

On May 8, 1793, the Government decided, subject to the sanction of Parliament, to issue

---

[1] It persevered therein, notwithstanding the change in the rate of exchange with France in the spring of 1793. The gold which then entered England did not reach the Bank.

[2] He not only exercised his influence with the Government. He also gave practical assistance by sending as much gold as possible to Glasgow. This assistance arrived before the Government had decided to issue Exchequer Bills.

£5,000,000 of Exchequer Bills in sums of £100, £50, and £20.[1]

As was so frequently illustrated during the past century, the mere fact that an ample supply of cash was made available was sufficient to allay the panic. The number of applications amounted to 138 only, and the actual issue was confined to £2,202,000.

[1] The Exchequer Bills were issued in amounts of not less than £2,000 at any one time. The "Commissioners" appointed for this purpose in London (for the provinces the collectors of taxes in Bristol, Hull, Liverpool, Glasgow, Edinburgh, and Leith had been entrusted with this mission) were instructed to grant "loans" in the shape of the aforementioned Exchequer Bills on security of merchandise which represented double the value of the sums advanced or on personal guarantee (other security) which was considered sufficient by them. These advances, together with interest at 5 per cent., had to be repaid at the Bank of England at least fifteen days before the Treasury Bills became due. If payment were not made in time, the deposited goods were sold by public auction. In cases where "other security" had been accepted the sureties were called upon.

The facility of obtaining advances against goods was only used to a small extent, because the opinion prevailed that the warehousing of the goods would exercise a prejudicial effect on their sale. The State sustained no losses as a result of its intervention.

In Liverpool the Corporation decided on May 10th to issue notes with the sanction of Parliament—"negotiable notes secured on the estate of the Corporation to the extent of £200,000" (cf. Macpherson, iv., p. 269, et seq.).

Thus the Government and a Municipal Council—that is to say, the public authorities—assumed the responsibility of the merchants, and created confidence by themselves showing confidence with respect to the gradual liquidation of their future capital. The resolutions of the merchants regarding the country banks had a similar tendency.

Meanwhile, the influx of gold from France continued, and towards the close of the same year the rate of interest in London had fallen below 4 per cent.

Once more the difficulty of obtaining specie had caused the panic, and those farthest removed from the great central store of " bullion " had the greatest struggle.

The blow dealt by the crisis of 1793 to the commercial and financial world was not merely transitory ; the market did not recover from it. Moreover, the times were unpropitious. Hostilities had begun between England and France, which, with intervals, continued for about twenty years and cost the country hundreds of millions.

It was a struggle for supremacy ; and the Government of the moment recognised the necessity of struggling with all its might. No efforts or expense must be spared lest England's cause be doomed to failure from the outset. Money was the primary requirement, and Pitt considered it in the best interests of the country to use all possible means to meet the war expenditure.[1]

---

[1] By order of the Government, the " assignats " which were issued in France during the war were forged wholesale in England, and it was Pitt's intention to introduce these forged documents on a large scale into France, and in this way not only to reinforce England's finances, but at the same time to prejudice the country with which he was at war (see for the historical description hereof Maberly Phillips, pp. 60, 61).

Unfortunately, the most obvious expedients were closely connected with the welfare of the English money market.

During the eighteenth century the Bank of England had strictly observed the limitations imposed upon it by the original Charter of 1694. Against its liabilities at short notice it kept assets, which did not consist of unrealisable or inconvertible capital, as so frequently occurred with the banks in the provinces. Its advances to the Government were repaid out of the proceeds of the taxes as they came in. Other transactions by which the Bank supplied capital were to a large extent represented by bills of exchange, and a small proportion only of its assets consisted of securities. Its cash reserve was subject to great fluctuations.[1]

[1] Its reserve of cash, bills held, and advances made to the Government stood at—

	Cash Reserve.	Bills.	Average Advance to the Government.
March, 1793 ...	£3,508,000	£4,817,000	£8,735,290
„ 1794 ...	8,608,000	2,908,000	8,494,600
„ 1795 ...	7,940,000	2,287,000	9,773,700
„ 1796 ...	2,972,000	2,820,000	11,351,000
„ 1797 ...	1,272,000	2,905,000	10,672,490

The position shown by the Bank Return for February 28, 1797 was briefly as follows :

Notes in circulation	£9,674,780	Govt. securities ...	£11,714,431
Deposits	4,891,530	Other „ ...	5,123,319
			16,837,750
Liabilities	£14,566,310		
		Coin and bullion	1,086,170
			£17,923,920

The bad harvest of 1795 and the large specie shipments for war expenditure had considerably stimulated the demand for remittances. The exchanges moved persistently in a downward direction, and soon gold began to leave the country. In consequence of the diminution of the metallic circulating medium the note circulation of the Bank expanded. Its note issue had already greatly increased since 1793 in consequence of the disappearance of a large number of country banks and their notes.[1]

Gold began to be exported in September, 1795. It was not long before the demand for gold reached the Bank of England. The latter promptly applied the method hitherto adhered to. On December 31, 1795, the Directors resolved to restrict their credit facilities during 1796.[2] Notwithstanding this, gold continued to leave the Bank.

Whilst in August, 1798, the position was :

Notes in circulation above £5 and Bank Post Bills...	£10,649,550	Govt. securities ...	£10,930,038
Below £5	1,531,060	Other „ ...	6,419,602
	12,180,610		17,349,640
Deposits	8,300,720	Coin and bullion ...	6,546,100
Liabilities	£20,481,330		£23,895,740

See Tooke, i., pp. 205, 207, and Macpherson, iv., pp. 411, 412.

[1] From August, 1794, until February, 1795, the aggregate amount of banknotes in circulation grew from £10,000,000 to £14,000,000.

[2] Although the amount of discount operations at the Bank

The idea, based indeed on the facts, had gradually gained ground that the Bank was a last resort when precious metal was needed ; as the number of banks increased throughout the country the demand made itself more urgently felt with each subsequent crisis. The greater the pressure the more the Bank of England thought of means to protect itself against such demands. The maintenance of an adequate cash reserve, as a means of self-preservation, became of paramount importance to the Bank. The requirements of the public constituted, in its eyes, a matter of secondary interest ; it did not recognise that in view of the central position which, in the course of time, it had come to occupy, a different interpretation of its mission might reasonably have been expected. It under-estimated the public confidence in its notes.

This question apart, the interests of the public and those of the Bank of England were certainly intimately associated, and by strengthening its own solvability the Bank at the same time furthered the interests of those who relied on it for support.

Meanwhile, Pitt's notorious proposal had, in 1793, become law ; [1] the Government freely

of England during 1796 did not fall far short of the total for 1795, yet it was to an ever increasing extent inadequate to meet the capital required by the merchants.

[1] The scheme submitted by the Bank to the Premier contained the stipulation that the Government would be free to

availed itself of its privilege. Moreover, loans of consolidated debt were issued, in which the Bank likewise participated to a large extent.[1] Its assets more and more lost their liquid character.

In 1794 the general situation at first was slightly improved, and the foreign exchanges moved in favour of the country. Gold, however, continued to leave the Bank, and the Bank persevered in the line of action it had once taken up. Towards the close of the year gold exports recommenced with renewed vigour.

Those who possessed gold kept it, having learnt by experience that "God helps those who help themselves." At the same time, other bankers had also adopted a more discriminating attitude in the matter of discounting. The result was a marked scarcity of circulating medium.[2]

The tension was still further aggravated by a poor harvest in the autumn of 1796 and by the severity of the succeeding winter. These circumstances precipitated the crisis.

The immediate cause of the outbreak of

borrow from the Bank of England without previously obtaining parliamentary sanction, "within a limited amount" viz., from £50,000 to £100,000. The Bill, however, was brought in without the limiting clause and passed by Parliament in that form.

[1] Cf. Clément Juglar, p. 304.

[2] As early as 1796 a meeting of merchants was held in the City in order to consider the critical situation, and to devise means to alleviate the pressure (cf. Tooke, i., p. 200).

the panic was, practically speaking, of minor importance. The crisis of 1793 began in London ; the crisis of 1797 originated in the provinces. In the early part of 1797 a French frigate landed a force of 1,200 men in Wales. The Government issued a decree to the effect that an inventory should be taken of all portable property belonging to the farmers residing near the west coast (their stock of cattle and their corn), and that it should be transported inland in order thus to compel the French to retire without inflicting losses upon the English themselves. The farmers wrongly interpreted this order. They became frightened. Those closest to Newcastle set the example by bringing their corn to town and selling it *à tout prix*. The proceeds were paid in notes, but they did not feel themselves safe with those, and immediately presented the notes at the respective banks for payment in cash, and kept the specie which they received.

Soon this course of action was generally adopted. The banks were obliged to pay in gold in view of the fact that the Bank of England refused to increase its note circulation, which prevented the country banks from keeping a reserve in banknotes. Then, too, it remains an open question whether the uneasy farmers would have contented themselves with Bank of England notes.

After a week full of anxiety, representatives of the banks in the North of England held a meeting on Saturday, February 18, 1797, and resolved, for the second time since their foundation, collectively to suspend the payment of their notes in gold. The public supported them in this action in the same way as it had done on the previous occasion, and guaranteed, by mutual arrangement, the continuance in circulation of the inconvertible banknotes.

The demand for gold spread from the provinces through the country bankers to London. Once again the Bank of England was called upon to render assistance. On the one hand, this institution persevered in its discriminating attitude with regard to the discounting of bills ; on the other, its notes were presented for payment in gold. On Saturday, February 25th, its cash reserve had shrunk to £1,272,000. It declared itself powerless to withstand the strain of its position any longer.

In contrast with the action taken in 1793, the Government now followed the example of the country bankers and compelled the Bank to suspend temporarily the payment of its notes.[1]

---

[1] Order in Council of February 26, 1797, followed by Act 37 Geo. III. c. 45. Simultaneously the Bank was authorised to issue notes smaller than £5, and the Act of 1777 which

What would have been a temporary measure in the case of private persons, who naturally would have endeavoured at the earliest opportunity to replace their business on a regular footing, became a permanent measure where the repeal of an administrative decree regarding a public institution was concerned.

Meetings were at once called in London, and also throughout the country, and resolutions were passed, in spite of many dissentient voices, declaring that all notes, whether of the Bank of England (in London the circulation of these notes alone was considered) or of the local banks, would be accepted in payment.[1]

The Scotch banks, too, had followed the example of their neighbours.

These successive crises are peculiarly interesting, because they throw light on the early phase of the organisation and development of the banking system in England. It may therefore be useful to recapitulate shortly the principal events :

1763. Crisis confined to London, especially to the commercial world. Caused

forbade bankers to issue notes below £5 was repealed. The provisions of this Act were extended to Scotland as well (Acts 37 Geo. III. c. 28, and 37 Geo. III. c. 32).

[1] As far as the Bank of England was concerned this decision was chiefly based on the large excess of assets over liabilities revealed by the return which it published by order of the Government.

the gradual extinction of the note circulation of the private bankers in London.

1773. The crisis is again confined to the commercial world, but leads to an extension of the circulation of the Bank of England notes beyond London. Simultaneously the doubtful policy of contraction of the note issue in case of an efflux of gold is adopted in principle by the Bank of England.

1783. The banks are so heavily involved in the events of the commercial and industrial world that for the first time the crisis may be characterised as a bank crisis. It is now apparent that the majority rely for support upon the Bank of England.

1793. The necessity for this support has become generally recognised, and the Bank is embarrassed to such an extent that the Government comes to its rescue and places State credit in the place of the credit of the Bank. The Bank, in consequence of its loans to the State, gradually encumbers its own position, and becomes so much embarrassed that in 1797 the renewed intervention of the Government becomes necessary.

> Then, whilst the whole country is in the throes of the crisis, and looks upon the Bank of England as its sole deliverer, the Government absolves the Bank from meeting its engagements.

With the Restriction Act of 1797 the basis of the central position of the Bank of England was firmly established. Twice in one decade the Bank had been saved from ruin by the Government. This afforded proof of the close relationship which existed between the two ; this relationship fortified the position of the Bank, whilst it strengthened public confidence in this institution. True, its notes were inconvertible, yet the impression that this was merely a temporary measure continued to prevail. Henceforward the bankers, including those in the provinces, kept their reserve chiefly in Bank of England notes.

The Bank had no longer any reason to limit the circulation of its notes. These gradually became more generally known in England and Wales, and when the Bank resumed specie payments its supremacy as a note-issuing bank had been established.

The period during which the Bank issued inconvertible paper money has been the subject of a great number of controversies. It created much ill-feeling, and many national calamities have been ascribed to one and the same fact. Prolific in events every one of which exercised its influence in one direction or another, this period afforded ample evidence for practically every conceivable economic theory. This opportunity has not been neglected. When, at a subsequent period, the banking system was to be recast by legislative action, both opposing parties based the arguments in support of their theories on the phenomena which had been produced in England at the commencement of the nineteenth century—both formed a school. Even at present this eventful period is difficult to understand, since almost every interpreter of the facts holds a different view.

The condition of the English coinage was again deplorable. Silver coins were of an inferior quality and clipped. The free coinage of silver had been prohibited in 1798,[1] but the Government did not meet the demand for heavy silver coins itself.

---

[1] 38 Geo. III. c. 59. The scarcity of silver made itself especially felt during the first years of the decade 1810-20. Already in 1797 "tokens" had been put into circulation by the Bank of England ; dollars on which the portrait of King George III. had been stamped served as English silver coins.

"Tokens" were no novelty in England. In the period 1642-72 they met the same wants as a century and a half later. Subsequently their issue was prohibited, but was again allowed by George III. in 1787. At that time the country was flooded with them, and in 1811 their issue was once more forbidden. Cf. Maberly Phillips, Chap. I., p. 37.

The Bank of England, moreover, adhered so strictly to the letter of the Restriction Act that even £5 notes were difficult to convert into specie. The London bankers experienced the greatest difficulty in accumulating coin in order to pay even smaller sums in specie.[1] At the same time Acts were passed in 1797 by which the issue of £1 and £2 notes were allowed.

No wonder that these notes soon became popular, and in 1798 the amount of such notes in circulation, as far as the Bank of England alone was concerned, amounted to £1,500,000.

Concurrently herewith England's trade and industry had considerably expanded during the first years of the last century, and this involved a renewed demand for capital. Banks sprang up in ever increasing numbers. The number of country bankers rose from 353[2] in 1797 to 900 in 1813.[3]

In London there were 68 private bankers

---

[1] Notwithstanding Art. 5. of the Act of 1797 (38 Geo. III. c. 1) authorised the Bank of England at its discretion "to advance, for the accommodation of the persons dealing as bankers in London, Westminster, and the borough of Southwark, in cash, any sums of money, not exceeding £100,000 in the whole."

[2] Cf. Thornton, loc. cit., p. 236.

[3] Shortly before 1814 all banks issuing notes were required to obtain a licence. In 1814 the number of applications for a licence on behalf of country bankers alone amounted to 940.

(of whom 22 were in the West End) in 1800, as against 83 in 1810.

With the exception of the London banks all of them were note-issuing banks, and their notes were readily received into circulation.[1]

The Bank of England supplied capital freely. Its note issue in 1798 exceeded the figure of the previous year by £2,500,000.[2]

In spite of the fact that the foreign exchanges had moved in favour of the country and that gold flowed into the vaults of the Bank so that the latter was soon in a position to announce its ability to resume specie payments, the Restriction Act was prolonged from period to period. Parliament feared that if the notes were again declared convertible, the gold which had come in from abroad would immediately leave the country again.

It was not until 1816 that the Government began to mint new silver coins.[3] At

---

[1] Maberly Phillips, p. 67 : "But time, the great healer, passed on. Money was wanted, which anybody by calling himself a banker could create, so that before the close of the century numerous new banks sprang up and money in the shape of notes was more plentiful than ever."

[2] Tooke, i., pp. 206–7.

[3] The bad conditions of the coins in circulation had caused a riot in Sunderland in the midst of the prevailing crisis.

The mint carried out its task with the utmost dispatch. Before June, 1818, half-crowns had been coined to the number of 11,908,000, shillings to the number of 50,490,000, and six-the same time the monetary system was placed on a firmer basis.[1]

The closing of the European ports against English goods led to extensive speculation. If the risks were great, the large profits in case of success fully outweighed them. In addition South America had been opened up as a result of the dethronement of the Braganzas in Portugal and their emigration to Brazil. When, in 1814, the continental system ceased to exist, there was increased anxiety to place English goods on the European markets, this time by legitimate means. But this put a stop to the remunerative smuggling trade which had been carried on during the preceding years.

Soon companies were formed on the " joint stock principle," and whatever capital was not obtainable from the public was to a large extent supplied by the banks which had just been established.

The crisis soon came. After wild speculation in 1813 and 1814 the calamities commenced in October of the latter year, continued throughout the year 1815, and culminated in 1816-17.

Eighty-nine country banks collapsed, and

pences to the number of 30,436,560 (cf. *An Account of Silver Coin coined in each Year since the Commencement of the Present System of Silver Coinage*, PP. 1828, vol. xvi., 434).

[1] 56 Geo. III. c. 68.

with them a large proportion of the fiduciary circulation came to an end. In respect of the banks which continued to exist a similar declaration was made as in preceding crises.

The Bank of England took advantage of the disappearance of its rivals. During the panic it freely issued its notes, being no longer bound by the rules formerly adhered to ; and when the crisis was over these notes took the place of the discarded country banknotes, although not to the same large amount.

The war on the Continent had been brought to a close, the gold standard had been adopted as the sole basis of the monetary system. The minting of the new coins had been completed, and they had been exchanged by the Bank for the " token money " which it had issued, whilst it had discontinued the issue of £1 and £2 notes. The average circulation of its notes amounted to near £20,000,000. When finally the Bank formally resumed specie payments in 1821 [1] its position, both in London and outside this city, had been strengthened to such an extent that

[1] Practically the Bank of England had begun to pay its notes in gold after the crisis of 1815–16. The crisis of 1818, which otherwise had no marked effect on the banking system, and the large gold exports which took place at that time, obliged the Bank, with the intervention of the Government, to suspend specie payments again. In 1819 the Resumption Act was passed, by which the banknotes were declared convertible as from 1823. As a matter of fact the Bank resumed specie payments before this date.

it looked as if Bank of England notes would entirely supplant the other fiduciary currency in England and Wales.

This seemed the more conceivable, since the country bankers had taken a further step in the direction of the consolidation of the English banking system. About 1814 the firm of Mowbray, Hollingworth & Co. opened a London house.[1]

From that time dates the ambition of the country banks to have an office of their own in the metropolis which might look after their London interests. Later it showed itself in other branches of business.

These tendencies have been to a certain extent offset by the establishment of branch banks in the country by the London banks, whilst in some cases the London house of the provincial bank after a time assumed the lead, and the original head office and its branches were made subservient to the London house.[2]

The country banknotes did not, however, circulate in London, and as the provincial banks were not admitted to the London Clearing House they acted the more readily as agents for popularising the notes of the Bank of England.

[1] In the list of "metropolitan bankers" for 1814 this firm is mentioned. The immediate cause was not improbably the admission of W. R. Stokes into partnership by the firm (Maberly Phillips, pp. 77–356).

[2] Thus, *e.g.*, Lloyds' Bank.

However, the tide turned. The serious calamities wrought by the crises of the past decade, the weak position of a number of country banks which was brought to light, their policy of giving credit injudiciously, and the consequent losses sustained by those who had placed confidence in them by accepting their notes—for all these evils the monopoly of the Bank of England was held responsible. Everything was ascribed to the fact that no banks could be erected either in London or in the provinces (with adequate working capital), whilst the Bank of England itself did nothing to meet the public needs by the establishment of " branch banks." It was urged that the clause in the Bank Charter by which the formation of banking firms having more than six partners was prohibited should be eliminated from that charter.

Once more an attack was made on the monopoly of the Bank of England. A timber merchant from the " Egypt " in Newcastle, a certain Thomas Joplin, placed himself at the head of the movement.[1]

[1] Egypt Raff (timber) Yard—so-called in 1796 " when so great had been the importation of grain into Newcastle that no warehouse room could be obtained for storing it and in consequence temporary wooden buildings were erected in a field adjoining the New Road, behind Sandgate, for 120,000 bushels " (Maberly Phillips, p. 90).

Joplin's views have been stated in his pamphlet *On the General Principles and Present Practice of Banking in England and Scotland* (*cf.* the *Pamphleteer*, vol. xxiv., No. 48).

Joplin had occupied himself for some time with the study of economic problems, and, as far as banking was concerned, he felt himself attracted towards the Scotch system. Whilst at the commencement of the nineteenth century numerous banks failed in England and Ireland, Scotland was spared all these evils. He thought this due to the fact that banks in Scotland were able to work with a large capital, which caused the number of shareholders to be larger, and made a closer supervision of the bank management possible, a supervision which the English system lacked.

Joplin did not place his light under a bushel ; he commenced his campaign in 1822,[1] and had the satisfaction of seeing the public and the Government side with him.

In the House of Lords the Government was interpellated by the Marquis of Lansdowne on the deplorable condition of Ireland owing to the great number of failures amongst the bankers, which he ascribed to the privilege of the Bank of Ireland.

---

[1] The direct result of his campaign was that numerous meetings on this subject were held. In 1823 he presented an address to the House of Commons requesting that an inquiry be made into the state of the "currency" and that steps be taken to improve the same.

When he came to the front the private banks of the country numbered about 1,000. At the present day their number does not reach 200.

The Government, represented by Lord Liverpool, replied that not only did they fully agree, and were considering an amendment of the law in Ireland, but that they desired the same modifications of the law for England as well.

The Bank of Ireland yielded, and in the same year the Irish Public Banking Act was passed. In 1823 the first joint stock bank was established at Belfast.

The Bank of England declined the Government's invitation, and adhered to its charter, which did not expire until 1833.

Circumstances came to the assistance of Joplin and his supporters.

Seldom were the after-effects of serious misfortune more severely felt than those following the crisis of 1825. The speculation by which it had been preceded, and which had been stimulated under the influence of the declaration of independence of the Spanish colonies in South America and Mexico, had affected the entire community in the same way as had been the case a century previously.

The flotation of companies for all possible and impossible purposes, all of them on the joint stock principle, had been the order of the day.[1] The number of country banks had

[1] To the capital requirements of private enterprises which "on paper" amounted to £372,173,100 were added the

reached a thousand, but the foundation on which they reposed was hardly firmer than that of their predecessors.

The attitude of the Bank of England was once again the cause of a panic. The precarious position which resulted from the speculation fever was, during a considerable time, bolstered up by the drawing and discounting of long bills of exchange, of which the Bank took its share. The Government Debt was being converted,[1] and the Bank again undertook to pay off those who were not prepared to take Four and Three-and-a-Half per Cent. Consols. To all this had to be added a gold export, which went on continuously from December, 1824.

For a long time the Bank of England did not take any efficient measures to stem the outflow of this precious metal. Its reserve shrank from £11,000,000 at the end of 1824 to £3,000,000 at the commencement of November, 1825.

Then, when its cash reserve had fallen to below £2,000,000 in the midst of the claims for capital of which it was made the centre,

numerous loans on behalf of various foreign States which in eight years reached a total of £52,994,571 (*cf.* Gilbart, i., pp. 62–64).

[1] In 1823 £135,000,000 5 per cent. Navy Bonds were converted into 4 per cent. Consols, whilst in 1824 £8,000,000 4 per cent. Consols were converted into 3½ per cent. Consols (Gilbart, i., p. 65).

the Bank resolved to discontinue its credit facilities. On November 23, 1825, the Bank began to discriminate in the discounting of bills and the making of loans.

Reaction followed almost immediately. The first failure occurred in York, at the beginning of December, and was followed, on the 12th of the same month, by that of the London house of Peter Pole & Co., who acted as " agents " for about forty country banks.[1]

General consternation ensued. Panic seized the public, and there was a " run " for gold.

Again the partners of the various banks left for London and endeavoured to secure gold, a mission which was fraught with extreme difficulty. The best bills and other securities were only partially sufficient.[2]

The failures followed each other in quick succession. The gold reserve at the Bank had nearly entirely disappeared. Then, for the

[1] "Bankers at Carlisle, Leyburn, Penrith, Richmond, Scarborough, Stockton, and Stokesley drew upon Sir Peter Pole & Co., and would all be seriously affected by their sudden stoppage." The crisis did not make itself felt everywhere to the same extent; the northern district was least affected by it (cf. Maberly Phillips, p. 92).

[2] As an illustration of the large quantities of gold required, the following passage may be quoted from the *Hertford Mercury* of December 25th : " Upwards of a million sovereigns passed through Ware on Saturday last and considerable quantities subsequently, as a relief to country bankers" (Maberly Phillips, p. 93).

third time, its notes saved the Bank from ruin.

This time it had not to rely on Government assistance ; at the most critical moment a box was discovered filled with £1 and £2 banknotes. These were eagerly accepted by the public, and this, added to the knowledge that the Bank was again ready to give assistance,[1] was the signal for a subsidence of the excitement ; the panic had been allayed.

The crisis of 1825 had set fire to the fuel which had been piled up ready to consume the privilege of the Bank of England. It was necessary that a scapegoat should be found for all the calamities of the last twenty-five years. This time the Government was firm in its resolution, notwithstanding the divergence of public opinion.

Notwithstanding the fact that the Bank Charter had not yet expired, the Government opened negotiations with the Bank, and energetically pushed them on. At the commence-

---

[1] The Bank of England persevered in its refusal to discount until Thursday, December 15th. It was not until then that it reversed its policy and adopted a liberal attitude. In the succeeding three days it issued £5,000,000 in notes (Gilbart, i. p. 65.)

The Bank had voluntarily discontinued the issue of £1 and £2 notes. The issue of notes below £5 had at the time been permitted to the country bankers as a temporary measure only for the period during which banknotes were inconvertible. In 1822 this term was extended to 1833 (cf. Gilbart, i., pp. 60 and 61).

ment of 1826 " the emancipation began of the English banks," [1] and was laid down in a series of Acts. The principal of these Acts was 7 Geo. IV. c. 46, which provided :

1. That note-issuing banks with more than six partners could be established, outside a radius of sixty-five miles from London ; their notes were not allowed to be issued nor to be made payable within this area.
2. That the Bank of England was authorised to establish branches.

At the same time, the issue of notes below £5 was prohibited definitely in England and Wales, whilst the existing notes of this class then in circulation were to be gradually withdrawn.

A yet more momentous change in the banking world was wrought by the discovery that a bank formed on joint stock principles, but carrying on business in the manner of the

[1] 7 Geo. IV. c. 7 : "An Act to facilitate the advancing of money by the Governors and Company of the Bank of England, upon deposits and pledges." The bills of lading and warrants would give to the holders a *prima facie* title of ownership to the goods specified in these documents.

7 Geo. IV. c. 6 : "An Act to limit and after a certain period to prohibit the issuing of promissory notes under a limited sum in England."

7 Geo. IV. c. 46 : "An Act for the better regulating co-partnerships of certain bankers in England."

London private banks, viz., a joint stock deposit bank, did not come under the exclusive clause of the Bank Charter Act of 1742. The law officers of the Crown consulted in the matter gave, as their opinion, that no legal objection existed to this view.

The Bank of England immediately approached the Government with the request that the clause of the Bank Charter containing its exclusive privilege should at once be amended and extended. The Government, however, was not prepared to comply with this request.

When the Bank Charter was renewed in 1833 it was specially stipulated that the exclusive right of the Bank of England merely applied to its privilege as a note-issuing bank. In the next year the London and Westminster Bank was established as the first London Joint Stock Bank. After a vigorous struggle against this new competitor, the Bank of England was finally obliged to give in and to accept the position of its adversary.

This recognition was the signal for the foundation of a number of other joint stock banks. Therewith began a new period in the history of English banking, during which the Bank of England has extended its business and has risen in public respect and appreciation, consolidating its position as a note-issuing bank, but at the same time has been compelled to confine its activity to the issue of notes and to its duties as Government banker and paymaster.

PART II

We have now passed under review a period which was the most important for the development of the English Money Market, viz., that during which the foundations of the English banking " system " were laid. The London bankers renounced their note issues, the Bank of England succeeded in gaining complete confidence, and the private bankers recognised that they could derive a twofold advantage from their situation. In consequence of the fact that they no longer issued notes, they were no longer exposed to the same extent to sudden demands for present capital—coin and bullion ; on the other hand, they were in a position to meet their engagements in Bank of England notes. This circumstance rendered the maintenance of an adequate store of present capital an essential duty for the Bank of England. It placed an additional responsibility on the Bank.

The notes of the private bankers were supplanted by another mode of payment. The cheque system grew up by the side of the Bank of England notes.

It has already been pointed out that the use of cheques does not offer great advantages, and is not open to expansion, unless a group of persons keep their deposits with the same banker. Usually this does not take place until the banker has become widely known and has enjoyed public confidence for several years.[1]

This requirement was, to a large extent, met by the custom of exchanging mutual claims, which has long been followed by the bankers. The establishment of the Clearing House, which further facilitated and perfected this exchange, made the new method of settlement a permanent institution.

It is the system of keeping accounts current which takes the place of the non-fiduciary circulating medium. Together with the exchange of cheques with which it is connected, it forms a system—the cheque system.

[1] *Cf.* Bagehot, Chap. III., *How Lombard Street came to Exist and why it Assumed its Present Form.* No general rule however, can be formulated in regard to this matter.

The Cheque Bank which was established in 1873 and existed for some thirty years could not be accepted as evidence of the contrary. The cheques of this bank might be placed on a par with banknotes of an international character. They were only issued against deposit funds, and the amount thereof constituted at the same time the limit which the cheques were not to exceed. For that purpose the amount which might not be surpassed was indicated on the cheque by perforation. Thus a depositor of £100 was entitled to receive, for instance, 100 cheque forms, each perforated for £1, which he could fill in for amounts of £1 or less.

The cheque only constitutes one part of the transaction by which capital circulates. Its counterpart is the transfer in the books of the banker.[1]

The transfer of a banknote implies the acceptance, by the receiver, of the note, *i.e.,* of the promise of a bank to pay.

This promise to pay is, in the case of a book-credit, comprised in the credit entry. The mere transfer of the credit entry to the name of the receiver of the cheque constitutes the acceptance of such promise to pay of the banker. As soon as this promise has been accepted, the banker is assured that he will retain for a brief period the capital which is entrusted to him.

Practically an identical transaction takes place when cheques which are drawn on one and the same bank—though they are not paid into the bank on which they are drawn, so that the amount of their face value would be re-deposited—nevertheless are not presented for payment by the various banking institutions where they have been paid in, but exchanged

[1] Or the payment in cash. In so far the cheque may be assimilated to the bill of exchange. But the bill is accepted, viz., the *drawee* signifies his acceptance of the agreement with the *drawer* and undertakes to pay the amount of the bill at a certain specified date. Thus the bill becomes future capital and may be circulated as such. If the cheque be accepted as is customary in the U.S.A., it likewise constitutes future, viz., short future capital which is equally suitable for circulation.

against counter claims on these institutions themselves. The credit which A, the drawer of the cheque, gave to his banker is taken over by B, the receiver of a cheque on another bank, who paid the same into A's bank.

By exchange of claims, the same amount of capital continues to circulate in the market which otherwise would have been represented by a similar amount of banknotes ; the names only of the holders of the short future capital are constantly changing.

As soon as this method of payment has been generally adopted the banker is again enabled to give credit on the lines originally followed in the issue of banknotes. Whilst formerly he gave short future capital in the shape of a tangible promise to pay, he is now placed in a position to grant credit to supply short future capital in the shape of an intangible promise to pay, viz., an entry in his books to the credit of the party concerned.

The manner of granting credit has changed by a circuitous process, but its character remains the same. The banker continues to make use of the future capital, since under the present system he is assured that the future capital supplied by him will at all times be accepted by some member of the community, so that no demands for present capital will be made upon him before the future capital ceded to him has been transformed into present capital.

This affords additional evidence of the fact that a banker remains an intermediary, and cannot supply more capital than is entrusted to him. But he anticipates now, to its full extent, any future increase of capital. He relies on the circumstance, that against those who are in need of present capital a group of persons exist who are equally numerous, and are sufficiently provided with present capital to be able to spare it for the time being. He does not wait until this has been specifically communicated to him. He is like a jobber,[1] who buys and sells when opportunity offers and relies on his ability to conclude a counter-transaction within a few days ; if the market is " free," the said jobber will probably buy against his sales on the same day that he sells, or sell against his purchases on the same day that he buys, and thus balances his books, as he cannot know what the morrow

---

[1] On the London Stock Exchange only members are admitted. These are divided into two groups. One of them, the "brokers," entertain relations with the public and transact business on behalf of their clients. The other, the "jobbers," are the intermediaries between the various "brokers." They carry on business under their own name and do not come into contact with the public at all. Their function, originally, at least, consists in finding a broker willing to buy from a broker desirous to sell, and *vice versa.*

will bring ; in a more limited market he will not be in such a hurry, as he counts upon a chance to effect the counter-transaction before the settlement, and prices of such funds are generally subject to slight fluctuations only. In the same way a banker will grant credit whenever he is requested so to do. He relies on the knowledge that fresh capital, in the shape of present or short future capital, will be entrusted to him on the same day apart from the expiring of credits previously granted, and that thus an equilibrium will be maintained.[1]

The secret of the daily money rates rests upon the degree of correctness of this calculation.

He may count upon this correctness with certainty as soon as a closer understanding has been established between the bankers themselves. When the public has once given confidence it continues to do so, except when crisis and panic deprive it of its reason and common sense. As long as business is good the public is satisfied with fiduciary circulating medium. It is not the customer who presents the notes for payment or withdraws the balance on current account—the notes are presented to one another by the rival bankers.

[1] Hence the custom of notifying the bank a few days in advance of the withdrawal of an amount of some importance.

In England, as in Scotland, an understanding was arrived at between the competing bankers with a view to promoting their mutual interests. Though they could not be expected to promote each others' note circulation, there was no reason why they should wilfully prejudice the same. A solution satisfactory to both was found in the settlement of mutual claims.

It would be difficult to state with certainty how long a period elapsed before the system of granting credit by book entry, by book credits, was adopted, after the cheque system had once begun to extend itself.[1]

It is probable that this method of giving credit had long been known, and that its origin, like that of practically every form of banking, might be traced to the Goldsmiths. In 1663 an entry appeared in the ledger of Alderman Backwell referring to a deposit by the then Queen-Mother Charlotte of £2,000 Navy Bills falling due six months later ; on the other hand, her account is credited with

[1] Probably it is connected with the development of the clearing system and would thus coincide with the admission of the joint stock banks and the Bank of England to the Clearing House and the institution of the "country clearing." The first joint stock banks were admitted as members in 1854, simultaneously with the adoption of the method of settling balances by cheques on the Bank of England. The latter was not allowed to share in the advantages offered by the Clearing House until 1864. Country clearing began in 1858.

their full face value, and it appears that she has disposed of this sum in instalments.[1]

It is not certain, nor is it essential, that she did so by means of cheques. This particular form of granting credit existed, but it may be reasonably assumed that it was not generally adopted until the development of the cheque system had reached a stage when it was completely adapted to the new method of payment and could form one system with it.

The use of this method was, for the time being, confined to the London bankers. Their notes were supplanted by those of the Bank of England, and the balances to be adjusted were settled in Bank of England notes.

Outside London, this system also gradually developed, in some districts independently of the Metropolis. In Lancashire, for instance, manufacturers and merchants drew bills of exchange on their debtors as well as on their bankers, on the latter against a deposit. The bills circulated, and were sometimes covered with several signatures. This method remained in vogue until after 1844.

The bills took the place of circulating medium.[2] The deposits were not always represented by cash deposits ; they frequently

[1] See p. 62, note 2.
[2] In London itself bills were still used as circulating media in the early sixties of the last century.

consisted in a credit entry in the banker's books. Probably this was also the origin of such a system of granting credits as that set out above, although the establishment of a branch of the Bank of England at Liverpool turned the custom into a different channel.[1]

The exchange of future against future capital did not reach its full development until the banknotes of the country banks began to inspire public confidence—the numerous failures during the closing years of the

---

[1] Tooke, vi., App. X., p. 579, offers the following remarks on the subject : " None of the banks in Liverpool issues notes. We have already stated in part the cause of this. The trade of the Manchester and Liverpool District gave rise to a large number of bills. The bankers found it more to their interest to re-issue the bills they had discounted than to issue notes. Such was the case until the Panic of 1825. The Bank of England then put down a branch at Liverpool and soon afterwards the joint stock banks were established here. The branch bank offered, as we stated, to discount for the joint-stock banks at 1 per cent. less than the rate charged to other parties, provided the banks would not issue notes nor re-issue bills. This arrangement suited both parties ; the branch bank got a circulation for its notes, the joint stock banks (whose customers always wanted capital) got their bills discounted at a rate which compensated them for not issuing either notes or bills, while they obtained a sort of connection with the Bank of England, which, at that time, was of importance to young banking establishments. The Act of 1844 abolished these bargains between the branch banks and other banks, but at the same time it prohibited these banks from becoming banks of issue. Hence, all the banks of Liverpool have necessarily remained non-issuing banks, and they have shown that banks may become wealthy and prosperous without having the power of issuing notes."

eighteenth and the first twenty-five years of the nineteenth centuries were not conducive to a strengthening of this confidence [1]—and until the country banks came to form part of the London system, by the establishment of agencies in the Metropolis, whereby they were placed in a position to settle mutual claims. This system had, roughly speaking, already been adopted prior to the year 1826,[2] but its full development only occurred subsequently.

The establishment of joint stock banks in the provinces was the great incentive to this development. These powerful institutions considerably increased in number during and after the prosperous years from 1833 to 1836, and practically encircled the whole country with a chain of branches. This was bound to lead both the method of remitting money and of granting credit along the lines indicated above, and to promote the consolidation of the various districts into one single banking system, the more so since the law of 1833 provided that country notes and bills below £50 could also be made payable at the issuing banks' agencies in London.[3]

[1] *Cf.* Maberly Phillips, *passim*, also the first appendix to his work.

[2] For example, the union between the banks in Northumberland and Yorkshire, more especially in Newcastle, which occurred simultaneously with the establishment of the Clearing House in London (*cf.* p. 237, *et seq.*).

[3] 3 & 4 William IV. c. 83, par. 2.

In addition, the establishment of branches in the provinces by the Bank of England since 1826, and by the London joint stock banks since 1833, supplied an additional stimulus.

These branches, in spite of their more recent formation, soon secured a commanding position.

In order to illustrate how this union grew systematically closer, a few general remarks may perhaps not be out of place.

The peculiar geological constitution of England's soil caused the various provinces to form themselves into distinct groups at an early date.

The mountain range, varied by moorlands, which runs from north-east to south-west, beginning in Northumberland and York and terminating in the southern extremity of Wales, divided the country into two halves— the north-west, where the rocky soil finds its continuation, and is merged into and terminates in the Scotch Highlands, and the south-east, which is comparatively flat and where comparatively large rivers form waterways, which place the remoter districts within easy reach of the outer world.

The political frontier between Scotland and England has been rather arbitrarily fixed from a geological point of view ; England's northern provinces have, from the earliest days, possessed peculiar characteristics, which they have preserved unchanged. Little adapted to agriculture, they were from the outset destined to devote themselves to commerce. The northern provinces are again divided into two parts by a branch of the same range of mountains, which, bending in an easterly direction, encloses in its two arms the country which is at present Lancashire but was once a marshy highland.

It was only in the middle of the eighteenth century that the remarkable development of this district began, assisted by the position and size of its ports, which made natural emporia for the American trade, whilst the growth of the American colonies, coupled with the important inventions of that period, formed the basis of its fame as an industrial centre.

The second group of this northern region is formed by Northumberland and Yorkshire. Their ports, **and** that of Hull, attracted from the earliest times the Baltic trade. The provinces constituted parts of the old Kingdom of Northumbria, which extended over the Lowlands of Southern Scotland.

The popular characteristics, morals, and customs in the main correspond with those of Scotland, and it is conceivable that in banking they gradually adopted what had already been customary for some time with their northern brethren, who resembled them both in race and in mind.

If this latter factor is taken into consideration when one examines the events of the first twenty-five years of the nineteenth century in England, it is not difficult to explain why the banking system developed along the lines which it actually followed.

This natural division necessarily affected banking. The system of limited companies, which during the decade 1810-1820 had vigorously pushed ahead, gave the crisis of 1825 a character resembling that of the " bubble " crisis of a century previously. In contrast to the rage for a division and limitation of liability, both in the domain of commerce and of industry, and the calamities by which the country was afflicted as a result of wild speculations and imprudence, the comparative quiet and insignificance of the disturbance caused in Scotland gave a favourable impression. The most salient feature in this connection was undoubtedly the better position in which Scotland was placed as regards a branch of business in which in England the joint stock system was entirely prohibited and in which the confusion was greatest. In Scotland four large joint stock banks existed, with a number of branches. These were in a position to assist the merchants in their difficulties and to avert many a disaster. In England, and especially outside London, such facilities not only did not exist, but the failures of the banks even aggravated the general confusion.

It can be understood under these circumstances that a keen thinker and able observer, such as Thomas Joplin, of Newcastle, though only a ship carpenter, was struck by the sharp contrast presented by conditions north and south of the Tweed and so near his home.

It can also be understood that he argued one-sidedly on the conclusions arrived at as a result of his observations, and that he threw all the blame of the excessive speculation and the consequences thereof on the system of banking followed in England. Again, it does not appear surprising to us that at such a time his words were readily listened to, and that he succeeded in organising a general movement against the exclusive privilege of the Bank of England.

Thomas Joplin never discovered the default, or rather the flaw, in the Bank Charter of 1742.[1]

If he had, this would have appeared from his writings, at least from his pamphlets and articles of the year 1822. In that year he laid stress on the desirability of the estab-

[1] Macleod's words crediting Joplin with this discovery have been literally reproduced in A. S. Michie's edition of Gilbart's book on Banking (ii., p. 152). *Cf.* Maberly Phillips, p. 88, *sqq.*

lishment of joint stock banks in England, and argued that no obstacle should be placed in their way ; following this line of reasoning, he argued that the Bank of England should be compelled by the Government to abandon its privileges in this respect.

In the same strain ran all the resolutions which were passed by commissions of bankers who combined to obtain official sanction to the foundation of joint stock banks, without closer definition of their sphere of activity ; and the petition presented to the Government in 1823 was couched in similar terms.

Joplin partly succeeded in 1826. We can now understand why at that time the establishment of joint stock banks remained unrestricted to that part of England which was situated outside the sixty-five miles radius round London, and why the Bank was induced at the same time to establish " branch banks." Northumberland did not fall within the radius, and the first branches were established outside this circle.[1]

The establishment of such branches had not been intended by the agitators ; hence strong opposition and numerous unsuccessful petitions.

[1] Manchester, Glasgow, Sheffield, Liverpool, Huddersfield, Birmingham, Dundee, and Norwich (see Gilbart, i., p. 60, also p. 70 and following with reference to the opposition of the country bankers).

After limited companies had once taken root in the banking world outside London and its vicinity, the time had come for this system to be merged with the credit system, which had now reached its full development, independently of the issue of banknotes.

We may leave on one side the question to whom the honour is due of having first pointed out that the provisions of the Bank Charter did not forbid the establishment of deposit banks on the lines of a limited company either in London or elsewhere in England.[1] The important point is that this discovery was made at a time when the community was ready to derive practical advantage from it. Before the Bank Charter had expired the prospectus was published of the London and Westminster Bank.[2]

After this digression regarding the banks in the north, we revert once more to the general discussion. As was the case in the north, the remaining counties south-east of the mountain range above referred to likewise possess their peculiar characteristics.

---

[1] As far as I have been able to ascertain Joplin's later works also contain no reference to this point.

[2] As no statutory regulations existed regarding joint stock deposit banks, and it was not specially provided that they should be subject to the same rules which applied to joint stock companies in general, all such banks were treated as Common Law partnerships. The difficulties resulting therefrom belong to a subsequent period.

They constitute England's agricultural districts. Owing to their continental trade the first to come into prominence were the Eastern districts in the vicinity of London. In Chapter I. it has already been pointed out that the wool trade was the mainspring of their prosperity, which proved to be a lasting one, and which gradually made these counties—with London as their emporium—England's commercial centre.

In the remaining districts the capital towns formed the centre of the surrounding country.

The extreme south-western counties, again, formed a separate group, by virtue of their American, and especially their African, trade, and of the fact that they are exceptionally suited for the equipment of fleets of war—for which purpose, in fact, the whole of the South Coast was, and still is, favourable.

The banks adapted themselves to the population and its mode of living. It was natural that they should form themselves into groups on the same lines as the people who were their customers.

These groups were little or not at all connected amongst themselves, but they all entertained relations with London.

When in due course branches were established by the more important of the new London banks in different parts of the country, these very branches became the basis of uniformity in the banking system, and led to the co-ordination of various banking groups which had existed side by side without much mutual intercourse.

The banks which established branches afterwards adapted themselves to the peculiar conditions prevailing in the districts in which they carried on business. But they had their head office in London. Thus the mutual relationship between the various provincial districts, with their diversity of interests, was assimilated with the mutual relationship of the head offices in London. As soon as these London banks were absorbed in the London banking system, this system became one uniform system for the whole of England.

The principal characteristic of the English money market is the decentralisation existing in the manner of granting credit, whilst at the same time the various banking institutions are closely connected by the placing of their actual reserve in the hands of one central note-issuing bank.

This system has frequently been the object of criticism, and often it has been suggested that the banks ought to cease to be mutually dependent on each other.

It has been shown that this system forms historically a whole. What in the course of time has slowly and gradually been welded into one whole it is difficult to put asunder by a few simple measures.

English banks have to fulfil a difficult task, and much is required from them, for they have become part and parcel of popular life. Every citizen has his bank as every citizen has his solicitor. All incidents which affect the citizens and which influence their actions, as far as their pecuniary interests are concerned, are bound to reflect themselves in their relations to their bankers. In a country like England, where the inhabitants are so intimately connected with all branches of industry and trade, where life is prolific in events, and, as a result of relations which extend over the whole world, influenced by almost every occurrence in any conceivable direction, it is desirable that, as far as such events affect the market for capital, the relations between the banking world and its customers should reflect as perfectly as possible any changes which may be produced by such events on the human mind.

The defects of an existing system are rarely to be found in the system itself. The nature of every existing system is to react as a whole on influences which directly only affect a part thereof ; otherwise it would not be a whole. If this quality be considered a drawback, there are but two remedies, viz., either to break with every " system " or to end all outward influences ; the former course would mean the loss of all advantages in the endeavour to suppress all evils, while the latter demands an alteration of human nature.

English common sense and cautiousness have adopted neither course. Matters are accepted as they are, but as experience has shown the weak spot of the entire system, the banking world constantly concentrates its attention on that point. It endeavours above all to strengthen that weakness in advance by taking timely action to insure that if at any time an occurrence outside the banking world causes a movement in the banking system, such movement follows as regular a course as possible.[1]

The fact that the cause of any such movement if it followed its ordinary course was, during the last two centuries, understood imperfectly or too late, was not attributable to the system, but to the men who had to handle it. Again and again so-called defects can be traced back to mankind itself, and the more the banking world becomes impressed with the truth of this the more intent it is upon thoroughly equipping those destined to assume the responsibilities inherent to its duties with

[1] Thus Fullarton concludes his argument against the currency theory by the following remarks : " We have chosen to make the Bank of England our sole depository of bullion ; we must abide by our election and have no reasonable line of policy left us but to endeavour to strengthen our hands."

the required knowledge and experience. It benefits by the experience of practical men and accepts the knowledge thus gained as a basis for its own, thereby ensuring co-operation, not only among the banking institutions themselves, but also among those on whom, as their employees, devolves the duty of carrying through all business connected with the banking profession.[1]

By the reserve is understood the quantity of present capital held in reserve to meet eventual demands in case future capital should no longer be accepted.

This should not be confused with what is termed " rest." The " rest " serves to replenish the working capital when a portion thereof has been lost, and also to maintain dividends as much as possible at a uniform level. This fund is not kept in the shape of present capital ; it is created and maintained out of yearly profits, but the money is generally employed in the current business or otherwise invested in first-class Government or other securities.

What is understood by " reserve " is kept by the banks in actual cash. Strictly speaking, this should consist of gold and silver

[1] The steps taken in this direction by the Bank of England are of comparatively recent date. The first practical result of these ideas was the establishment of the Institute of Bankers in St. Clement's Lane, E.C., in 1879.

either in specie or in bars. It has, however, already been pointed out that in the second half of the eighteenth century the London bank   discontinued the issue of their own note   The Bank of England notes enjoyed general confidence, and it gradually became customary for the London bankers to keep, apart from their stock of bullion, a certain amount of banknotes in reserve, as is customary in all countries where the issue of notes is exclusively in the hands of one central institution.

There is nothing to object to in this. As long as a bank enjoys public confidence— that is to say, as long as the bank is considered sufficiently strong to meet its engagements and to be in a position at all times to exchange its short future capital (in the shape of promissory notes) against present capital (in the shape of actual gold or silver)—the public is satisfied to accept these promissory notes in lieu of gold or silver. If a bank has never broken its word during a record career of two centuries, whether in times of prosperity or of adversity—be it on account of its own inherent strength or as a result of its being able to rely on a superior power which, even if the bank should find itself in difficulties and should consider the advisability of deferring the fulfilment of its obligations, it is understood, would on no

account suffer this to take place—if such
conditions have prevailed for so long a period,
the public is sufficiently satisfied as to the
bank's security, and the promissory notes of
such a bank will be as readily accepted as
present capital in the shape of coin.

That superior power is the State ; if the
State fall, it carries with it every national
institution. As long as the safety and
strength of the State are above suspicion,
its guarantee, though not given in writing
and only existing in the opinion which the
public has derived from practical experience
that the " promise " to pay shall be fulfilled,
will be as readily accepted as the State's
guarantee that the coins in circulation are of
a certain specified weight and contain a specific
quantity of gold and silver.

This is carried even farther. Even if this
latter guarantee should prove unreliable, confidence in the former would remain unshaken.
After the coins in circulation have, through use
and abuse, become worn out to such an extent
that actually they contain a portion only of
the metal which they are supposed to contain
—and if on this account their value decreases
and the public accepts them at their real value
only—even then the notes of the note-issuing
bank circulate without any difficulty or de-
preciation. They contain a promise to pay
a certain amount of present capital wnich

at the time of payment will correspond with the nominal sum specified on the note of a number of coins which represent a corresponding quantity of gold or silver, not of a number of coins which contain part only of the face value of the note. As long as, in reality, this promise is not discredited the public has no reason to doubt the fulfilment thereof.

This is most strikingly illustrated by the events of the eighteenth century, when Bank of England notes continued to circulate without being depreciated, in spite of the deplorable condition of the coinage. The Bank changed its notes in coins of full weight, since all terms were expressed in terms of the coinage, and, of course, had to be paid in coins which were not below the legal limit.

There is but one set of conditions which leads to difficulties in the circulation of the notes, and this is implied in the foregoing remarks. It occurs when doubts are entertained as to the bank's ability to meet its engagements, when—as it is called—confidence is shaken, and every holder of a note hastens to realise at once what he holds in the shape of future capital, but which can be changed into present capital at any time. Such moments the Bank of England has only experienced twice, the first time in 1696 and a second time in 1745, when the Pretender had advanced with his army as far as Derby and the safety of the State itself was despaired of. A similar panic had to be faced by the Goldsmiths in the seventeenth century, when the Dutch fleet, under Admiral de Ruyter, burned Chatham. In such circumstances, present capital only has any value.

Taking this into account, a central circulating bank may, besides its reserve in present capital, keep a reserve in its own notes,[1] viz., it may be so much convinced of public faith in its own institution that it is able to estimate within what limits its notes will continue to circulate, and go on issuing notes within such limits.

Banknotes remain in circulation, and are not presented for payment—except for small change.[2]

[1] Although this thesis may appear paradoxical its meaning will be illustrated by what follows in the text. As long as a bank takes care always to maintain an adequate and corresponding reserve in gold and silver, it may together with it expand its note issue indefinitely for such requirements as arise and as are equally well met by notes as by gold and silver coins. In the case of the Bank of England these notes in reserve are represented by bullion in the Issue Department, as the Bank of England is not entitled to issue notes beyond a certain maximum unless such additional issue is covered by an equal quantity in gold.

[2] This is clearly apparent from the returns of continental note-issuing banks which are published annually with their Annual Report. It is corroborated by the many years' experience of the authorities of the Bank of England. In case gold be required for export it is withdrawn from the Bank directly on a deposit account or against corresponding values which are

As soon as banks are established in a country, this fact will create elasticity of the circulation—that is to say, the amount of currency in circulation regulates itself, in accordance with the requirements of the public, which fluctuate from week to week and from year to year.[1]

As long as metal currency alone circulates in a country, the elasticity expresses itself in the import and export of bullion only. Once banks have been established, the surplus quantity for which there is no immediate demand will find its way into the vaults of these institutions in the country itself.[2]

Demand for gold and silver may be caused either by requirements for internal circulation or for export abroad.

The former are governed primarily by

handed over to the Bank and generally consist of future capital (advances against securities or against bills which are discounted). The mere fact that exports of gold run into considerable amounts and would require the accumulation of a considerable number of notes, makes it improbable that gold should be demanded for notes. As a result of the division of the Bank of England into two departments the transfer of the notes from the Bank to the Issue Department takes place independently of the person who requires the gold. And why in ordinary times should notes return to the Bank—in large numbers at least—in order to be exchanged against gold, if it were not for purposes of export of gold? Practice fails to supply an answer to this question. Cases of an internal panic arising from loss of confidence in a bank or bankers are not included in the expression "ordinary times." *Cf.* further p. 246, *et seq.*

[1] *A Century of Banking in Dundee*, p. 1.   [2] See p. 164.

the requirements in connection with ornaments, &c. ; these are chiefly met by import
of gold and silver from abroad. Where these
wants are satisfied by the melting of coins,
such procedure diminishes the currency in circulation, and the demand then changes into
the second form in which internal demands
make themselves felt, viz., that for circulating
medium. We have seen that the latter
demand—except as regards the smaller coins
—may be equally well satisfied by banknotes. The maintenance of a reserve for
internal demands does not require any special
provision ; and if this demand alone had
to be taken into consideration, the question of the reserve would not, indeed, have
given so much concern.

It is the export to foreign countries, it is
the foreign exchanges, which in every banking
system and to every note-issuing bank present
the chief difficulties—the demand for present
capital, which cannot be met by short future
capital nor by capital in any other shape but
coins and bullion. The banks have gradually
absorbed the entire stock of gold and silver
which is not immediately required for pressing
internal demands. Consequently it is they
who, in case of adverse exchanges, are called
upon to supply the necessary capital.

We must now consider to what extent such
demand affects the English money market.

Our historical review has been continued far enough for our purpose, for since 1826 the centralisation of the reserve has not changed, though it has been intensified.

In the course of the eighteenth century the Bank of England had become the holder of the chief reserve of bullion in England. The London bankers had discontinued the issue of notes. The fact that they held Bank of England notes in their tills increased the responsibility of the Bank. The bankers themselves did not entertain direct relations abroad. Unfavourable foreign exchanges could not directly injure them. The country banks maintained a comparatively small cash reserve.

A special demand for cash in the provinces led through them to a corresponding demand for cash from their agents. The demand passed afterwards to their London houses, and through these again to the Bank of England.[1]

The difficulty of obtaining metal was probably one of the causes which induced these London firms to leave a balance with the Bank of England, so that in case of emergency they could always obtain from it either notes or coins. This procedure became more

[1] The Scotch and Irish Banks, too, were always without adequate cash resources. It has been pointed out already how towards the close of the eighteenth century Scotland sought for cash in London.

general as the circulation of notes of the Bank of England gradually extended over the whole of England, and was confirmed by the admission of the Bank to the membership of the London Clearing House in 1864.

In 1816 England adopted the gold standard. From this it followed that, even if the Bank should hold both gold and silver in reserve, gold would hold the upper hand. As soon as its notes were again convertible, the Bank was obliged to exchange them against such currency as was legal tender.

At that time there still existed one other source from which it was possible to obtain gold, a source which has since almost completely dried up ; gold could be collected from the circulation. True, the quantities thus laboriously scraped together were but small, yet by continued efforts they formed a fairly large amount. In countries where the cheque system has not yet fully penetrated, and where it is not customary for practically every member of the community to place his superfluous cash with his banker, this method of collecting gold is still in vogue.[1]

[1] Struck, *Skisse des Englischen Geldmarktes*, p. 59 : "It not infrequently happens that, when the Bank of England raises its rate of discount in order to attract gold, the central banks abroad which are not in a position to part with any gold without endangering their own reserves soon follow the example of the Bank of England in order to protect themselves and in their turn increase their rates of discount. Nevertheless

But to deprive the classes without banking accounts of their circulating medium may be considered identical with a deprivation of the central bank itself of the same. For in normal times these amounts remain in circulation and flow through the intermediary of those who do keep banking accounts, into the hands of the bankers, and through them into the central bank, in order to be withdrawn again from the central bank by these bankers and returned by them into circulation ; to speak metaphorically, these funds flow through the central bank.

In times of tension this ceases. Whatever flows into the central banking institution is

we find that after a certain time gold flows from abroad to England and that the central banks allow the same to leave the country without making further efforts to retain it. This change in the attitude of the foreign central banks towards the question of gold exports must be ascribed to the fact that they have succeeded by the higher rate of interest in attracting gold from internal circulation. Thereby they have secured more than they require, and they are in a position without risk to themselves to give up the surplus to the Bank of England, which requires it." Again, p. 13 : " One can further consider the stock of coins and notes in the hands of the classes which have no banking connection. This stock is evidently greater than the actual circulation requires. . . . In any event the quantity of coins and notes in the hands of these classes is not a fixed one, but fluctuates, now increasing, then diminishing. . . . For that reason the money market cannot count with any degree of certainty nor permanently on its ability to fall back upon the coins and notes in the hands of the classes outside the banking system. And it will only rarely be able to expect any very important assistance from this quarter."

retained there, and it will be necessary to apply to it directly in order to secure gold or silver coin.

Hence, even at that time, every demand for gold was concentrated on the Bank of England or in the open market. It would now hardly be remunerative to attempt to accumulate any considerable quantity of gold from the amount of currency in circulation, or to exercise any pressure to secure it in this way ; there is a sufficient amount of gold in circulation, but the amount is in proportion to the requirements.

Neither does the open market form a reliable source for the satisfaction of demands for coin. The available data for a description of the historical development of the bullion market are insufficient.[1] One is obliged to confine oneself to the conditions which have prevailed since the passing of the Act of 1844.

Mindful of the fact that the British legislator seldom creates, but mostly sanctions, it seems reasonable to assume that these conditions had already existed prior to that year, and were then legalised.

The gold which is offered in the open market is either obtained from the internal circulation by the melting down of coins into bars, or from abroad in bars and specie. The

[1] That is to say, as far as they have been made public.

proportion of the former is—since the Coinage Act of 1816—comparatively speaking, insignificant.

According to the provisions of this Act, the Bank of England is obliged to buy standard gold (eleven-twelfths fine) at £3 17s. 9d. per ounce. One ounce of gold gives £3 17s. 10½d. minted. Although no charges are made for minting, the person who brings gold to the Mint suffers loss of interest during the time required for minting. The result is that private persons rarely sell the gold which they do not require for other purposes, except to the Bank of England.

The fixed purchase price of the Bank has the effect of limiting the fluctuation of the price of gold on the bullion market to one-sixth per cent.—that is to say, the difference between £3 17s. 9d. as the minimum and £3 17s. 10½d. as the maximum price. If the market price rises above £3 17s. 9d. per ounce, holders of gold will immediately dispose of their stock. The gold then sold may safely be exported without troubling the Bank of England.

If, on the other hand, the demand is limited and no purchaser can be found for the imported gold, then the holder has the option between retaining the gold until demand arises, in the hope of securing a more favourable price than the price paid by the Bank of

England, and straight away selling it to the Bank.

If he waits, he suffers loss of interest. The sum realised by selling it to the Bank of England could immediately have been remuneratively employed, be it only as a deposit with one of the banking institutions. By waiting, he can never gain more than one-sixth per cent. At a rate of interest on deposits of 3 per cent., a capital of £3 17s. 9d. yields $1\frac{1}{2}$d. in twenty days. Beyond twenty days it would in any case be unprofitable to wait. The market price does not rise above £3 17s. $10\frac{1}{2}$d. If it remains lower, the period shrinks during which waiting may secure some profit. The same is the case if the rate of interest on deposits is higher than 3 per cent. ; if it is lower, the period naturally expands.

If it be taken into consideration that, after all, these are extremely insignificant fluctuations in a future price which cannot be ascertained in advance with any degree of certainty, it may be safely assumed that all the gold which is imported, and not immediately bought up for re-export, flows into the Bank of England, and that the open market is never supplied with a stock of gold of any importance.[1]

Every demand for gold in England, both

---

[1] Struck, *loc. cit.*, p. 15, *sqq.*

internal and foreign, reaches the Bank of England. The Bank holds the ultimate reserve of the English money market, and it will continue to do so as long as no difficulties are encountered by the English banking system in its development along the road marked by history ; and the Bank of England will retain this position even if the banks should decide to maintain large cash reserves themselves instead of depositing these mainly with the Bank of England, where they figure amongst the Bank's " deposits " under the heading of " Bankers' Balances."

It is in this way that the position of the foreign exchanges affects the English banking system. That system is purely a national one. The central position which London now occupies in the commerce of the world has been built up during the nineteenth century. It was only after the provisions of the 1833 and 1844 Acts that England's money market through " foreign bankers " and " foreign brokers " became closely connected with the money markets of other countries, and that the Bank of England became affected even by shipments of bullion which did not concern England at all.

If the reserve of the Bank of England becomes affected, this does not directly endanger the position of the remaining banking institutions. The Bank begins, however, to be more cautious in its credit operations. It has already been shown that towards the close of the eighteenth century it adopted a special course to protect its reserve without taking into consideration whether the demand for coin and bullion was confined to internal requirements or whether it was connected with movements abroad. It was not until the middle of the nineteenth century that it began to discriminate between the two. " Country banking " has considerably improved since 1826. The banks have become more closely connected with each other, and the whole system has grown more systematic. The internal gold movements have in consequence gained in regularity, and at present it is almost possible to determine them in advance for the current year with complete certainty. This could not fail to be recognised by the Bank itself. In addition to this there must be taken into consideration the great dispute on " Banking Theory," which in no wise left the foreign exchanges undiscussed. It is certain that since the Act of 1844 the Bank of England has paid closer attention to commercial relations with foreign countries as far as these are reflected in the foreign exchanges.

Whenever the Bank of England contracted its credit facilities the London bankers were compelled to follow its example, for they were not in a position to continue granting credit unrestricted, when the certainty that they could always cover themselves had ceased to exist.

They in their turn caused the provincial banks to experience greater difficulties in securing the same credit facilities as they had done previously. If the London banks obtained credit less willingly, they in their turn had to restrict their credit facilities to others, and curtail their loan operations.

Thus it appears that an export of bullion which caused a serious decrease of the gold reserve of the Bank of England created a situation akin to that in time of a crisis. But in a time of crisis the impulse frequently originates in the country, and only ultimately reaches the Bank of England.

It is, however, an economic law that if the demand increases when the supply remains the same, the fact has the same effect as a decrease of the supply when the demand remains unchanged. In both cases the demand is not satisfied.

There is, however, one fundamental difference between the two. Demands from abroad must be ultimately met by gold. Internal currency requirements need not be satisfied by coin. And since the country bankers are only bound to consider the needs of their immediate customers, gold exports do not—directly—concern them much. Their bills are drawn on

London, and through London their accounts
with other districts are adjusted. It is only the
close cohesion of the component elements
which causes a shock experienced by any one
of them to be felt throughout the entire system.

The provincial banks keep notes of the
Bank of England in reserve ; and the way
in which they chiefly secure these is through
their London agents. As the merits of
transit increase in velocity their own cash
reserves are gradually curtailed, whilst they
increase their deposits in London. The possibility of having at any time a quantity of
notes at their disposal takes the place of the
reality, viz., the possession of the notes themselves, and forms an extension of the period
for future capital.

During the few years immediately preceding 1820 the note circulation of the
country banks had shrunk considerably. Mr.
Lewis Lloydd [1] was of opinion that this should
be ascribed to the currency requirements in
the country districts. Though these caused a
demand for the notes of the country banks, the
notes did not remain in circulation. As soon
as they came into the hands of a sister institution they found their way to London, there

---

[1] London agent for, and partner in, Jones Loyds of Manchester, in his evidence given before the Commission of the
House of Commons in 1819 (cf. the Report of this Commission
1819, iii., p. 164 and following).

to be exchanged against Bank of England notes.

In addition, he considers it a result thereof that an arrangement was made between the banks mutually to exchange each other's notes, in order to prevent their being sent to London.

In some of the counties this custom had already been adopted at an earlier period, viz., by those counties which were situated close to the Scotch border. This is the more characteristic, as the Scotch banks themselves had since the middle of the eighteenth century followed a system of exchanging each other's notes.[1]

Before 1788 a properly constituted association of bankers existed in Newcastle, with articles and regulations which were adopted by mutual agreement, and which related to the settlement of their liabilities.[2]

At the same time, it seems to have been customary among them to present for payment at regular intervals [3] to the issuing banks such of their notes as had passed into the hands of the various other bankers.

[1] In 1752 the Bank of Scotland and the Royal Bank adopted the system of note exchange which has (with modifications) continued to the present time (A. W. Kerr, p. 67).

[2] For the history of this Association cf. Maberly Phillips, p. 116 and following, and note the examples quoted therein. For a description of this custom and the advantages derived therefrom, see Gilbart, ii., p. 187 and following.

[3] In order to secure as much uniformity as possible in the amounts.

These were as much as possible exchanged by the bank to which they were presented against notes issued by the bank presenting them for payment. The balance was adjusted by a cheque on London.

It was merely a custom, and the banks were not obliged to adopt it, but if they departed from the usual practice complaints were at once raised.[1]

Between 1788 and 1825 nothing further is heard of this custom ; it seems to have been continued in the manner which had once been adopted. Undoubtedly frequent departures were made from this rule in cases where the balance was claimed in gold, and this fact, coupled with the above-mentioned circumstances to which attention has been drawn by Lloydd, appears to have strengthened the desire that fixed rules should be made in this respect also. At any rate, shortly after 1826 the bankers in the northern counties decided

[1] Bitter complaints were made against Mr. Benjamin Dunn, banker, at Durham, Messrs. Surtees, Burton & Co., Newcastle, and others, because they would demand gold in settlement. The following letter, dated March 19, 1790, shows the custom of settling weekly, and also proves that no fixed rules existed for settlement :

"Baker, Hedley & Co. (Commercial Bank, Newcastle) present their compliments to Messrs. Lambton, Williamson & Co. In future they would wish the balance of the weekly statements to be paid either in Gold or in a Bill at ten days on London, and five shillings per cent. carriage, in the option of the Payers." (Maberly Phillips, *op. cit.*).

to come together at fixed periods in order to settle their demands at short notice. These " clearings " took place weekly or fortnightly, and were similar in character to the " settlements " in the London Clearing House, although slightly differing from the latter in consequence of the difference in the nature of these demands.[1]

The balance was adjusted in gold or in Bank of England notes. This had become possible since the Bank of England had opened a branch bank in Newcastle. In 1837 meetings were held in a room of the Northumberland, Durham, and District Bank.

Meanwhile the opposition against these " branch banks " had died down, and bankers had realised that it was desirable, if not essential, to co-operate with institutions which had justified their existence. Instead of holding the meetings in the room above referred to, it became customary soon after 1837 to effect the settlement with the " branch bank."

---

[1] Mr. Burgess, in his " Circular to Bankers," March 20, 1829 : " Since the panic of 1825, a meeting has taken place once a week or once a fortnight at Northallerton (previously at Thirsk for a short time) at which bankers from Stockton, Darlington, Richmond, Ripon, Knaresborough, Thirsk, Boroughbridge, &c., attended. And this meeting, we are informed, has been most useful, instructive, and agreeable. It is a little centre of exchange for the bankers of that part of the country, where demands upon each other are cleared as at the Clearing House in London, but in a somewhat different manner, the transaction being so different " (Maberly Phillips, *op. cit.*).

In this respect the provinces set an example which was only followed in London a quarter of a century later. The various bankers kept an account current with the " branch bank." Every day at a certain hour each of them sent all cheques and notes which he held on the other banks to the " branch bank," and the amount thereof was placed to his credit in the books of the latter. Before closing time a clerk of the " branch bank " went the round of the various institutions on which the demands were made out and received payment in Bank of England notes or by cheque drawn on an account current with the " branch bank," which further saw to the adjustment of the various claims and counterclaims in its books.[1]

This system was subsequently modified according to circumstances, and led to the establishment in 1872 of a separate Clearing House in Newcastle, which after 1882 also included the bankers of the surrounding locality. All balances were now adjusted by cheque on the branch Bank of England. Thereby the more cumbersome method of "country clearing," introduced in London in 1858, had become superfluous for those places as well as for Manchester, without its being necessary to infringe the system of settlement in the books of the Bank of England.

We have pursued this history right to its

[1] *Bankers' Magazine*, 1845, p. 219.

close, beyond the scope of this work, in order to demonstrate more clearly that the desire for organisation was not merely of London origin, but passed through various stages of development in the provinces as well as in London. In Lancashire a similar system had sprung up, which in an identical manner led to the establishment of the Clearing Houses in Manchester and Liverpool.

In these places bills circulated instead of notes. The drawer of the bill kept an account current with his banker, sometimes created by a deposit of present capital, but generally by the taking of a " loan." The bill was drawn for three months or longer,[1] and when it fell due the settlement took place between the banker who held it and the one on whom it was drawn. The method of payment in this case was a combination of the system on which the cheque is based with that of the note circulation. In the decade from 1810 to 1820, as in all periods of adversity and commercial distrust, the banknotes gained in popularity, and after the establishment of

[1] They circulated in amounts from £5 to £5,000, £8,000, and £10,000. "The Banker has only to do with his customer : the customer applies to his banker for such a bill as he wants, the banker keeps a regular interest account with his customer, and the customer is debited only with that bill on the day it falls due, so that he is not charged with interest till the bill is due" Lloydd's evidence (*House of Commons Committee*, 1819, iii., p. 169).

branch banks by the Bank of England the circulation of bills became superfluous,[1] though this system has still been known to the present generation. It was only completely supplanted by the development of the cheque system.

A peculiar feature of the bill circulation was that the currency thus created was derived from those to whom it had to serve as currency, viz., the public. The possibility that the currency in circulation exceeded the requirements was thereby excluded.

The bills were only drawn when capital was required. They fell due at specified times. If occasionally more bills were held by some persons than were wanted for immediate use, these bills as a rule returned without delay to the banks, either as a deposit or for discount by the drawees.

Present capital is always worth more than future capital. When, however, in times of prosperity, the certainty increases as to the gradual and satisfactory liquidation of the transactions concluded for a future period— when confidence remains unshaken and

---

[1] "It has been chiefly owing to the accommodation latterly afforded by the Bank of England to the country banks, and the free supply of its notes on easy terms, through its branches, for the provincial circulation, that the use of bills in Lancashire as money has for some time been progressively on the decline" (Fullarton, *On the Regulation of Currencies*, 1844, p. 47. *Cf.* p. 49).

present capital fully meets all requirements—
then the premium of present as compared to
future capital falls to such an extent that
bills having three months or less [1] to run
circulate as currency without deduction of
discount, whilst eighteen months' and two
years' bills are readily discounted. As soon
however, as depression sets in, present capital
rises in value, and confidence decreases, so
that even short bills are offered for discount.[2]

Credit in every form may serve as circulating medium ; its discount as against
present capital will depend on the trouble
connected with its conversion into present
capital. As a standard of value no form
of future capital can be employed ; as such
present capital alone has value, and then in
the shape of precious metal only.

London has become the centre of the credit
system of the whole of England. We saw
that most of the country banks had an
agency in London. It has been shown
that the balances between the different banks
were adjusted by bills on London. On the

---

[1] This period of three months corresponds with the average
time for which the Bank of England notes remain in circulation,
viz., ninety days.

[2] Lloydd's evidence before the House of Commons Committee :
" No doubt there is a great number of bills now [in 1819, March]
seeking discount which in a different state of things would have
passed as circulating medium without being offered for discount."

other hand, it was difficult for banks in some parts of England to find suitable banking investment for the funds deposited with them ; whilst in districts such as Lancashire the number of bills offered exceeded by far the number of bills received.

A bank cannot lend more capital than it receives. In those districts it became customary for the banks to rediscount their bills. They were sent to London and taken by the agents of those banks who wanted investment for their surplus funds. Thus the surplus capital of one district in England flowed, via London, to those parts where it was most needed.

In these operations lay the reason for the rise of the bill brokers. Their history falls entirely into the succeeding and final period.

CONCLUSION

OUR study of the development of the London money market has shown us the place which the banking system has gradually taken in the process of production and distribution of goods.

A bank's method of supplying capital can no longer be compared with the function of a shopkeeper, who is an intermediary between the wholesale producer and the consumer. It places those in need of capital in a position to find what they require—viz., present capital —in the open market.

A bank becomes both the creditor of its customer, by the granting of a loan, and the debtor, by the payment thereof in notes. The person who receives the notes transfers these in exchange for goods to a third person, who thus in reality supplies the credit.

In this way a bank becomes, to a large extent, independent of the present capital with which it is entrusted. That capital may be employed for other purposes. As it exists in the shape of precious metals, it will, as a rule, if not required for home industry, be exported.

The place of the present capital which constituted the currency is taken by the bank's future capital.

A bank can do this as long as (1) it enjoys
public confidence, and (2) there is sufficient
present capital available in the country to serve
as a basis of the credit operations.

The first condition is not altogether under
the control of a bank. To keep itself well
informed of the circumstances constituting the
second condition forms its specific duty.

A bank can never keep notes in circulation
in excess of the number required. Those in
excess will return to their place of issue.[1]

[1] The old theory was that they did return, but in exchange
for coin and bullion. The father of this theory, which is certainly not true under present circumstances, was Adam Smith
(*Wealth of Nations*, ii., chap. ii., p. 239). Smith probably based
his judgment on the conditions which prevailed in the Scotch
banking world. It is, however, a well-known fact that Scotland has never known a large stock of bullion. The majority
of banks were note-issuing banks only. The fact that even the
larger banks were reluctant to part with coin and bullion, and
only did it when compelled to do so by the presentation of
their notes, and even then endeavoured to render this obligation as little burdensome as possible, is clearly illustrated by
the "optional clause" in their notes. This clause contained
the provision that the banknotes were to be "payable at
demand or —— days (months) after sight." If, under such circumstances, metal was required for shipment, there was no
alternative but to accumulate notes and present the same for
conversion into bullion at the bank which issued them. To
accumulate gold from the circulation by offering a premium
would have been of little purpose, since the stock of coin was
already such a small one.

In the northern counties a similar "optional clause' became
customary, with the addition that the notes were to be payable
in London only. Maberly Phillips, on p. 45 and following,
mentions a note of the firm of Backhouse & Co., dated 1779,
a five-guinea note, "where they undertake to pay upon demand
or twenty-one days after sight at Messrs. Smith, Wright and

A bank's assistance is generally required in the final stage of the period of production. If a bank, under the circumstances, has been too liberal in granting credit facilities it will itself suffer most.[1]

A loan is never asked for unless present capital is required. The notes (future capital) supplied by the bank in granting the loan are immediately employed in the ordinary course of business. They return to the bank either in repayment of the loan, or if no longer required in circulation. In that case they will return, though not in exchange for coin or bullion, if—

(a) the bank has a monopoly, and if

(b) it is at the same time a deposit bank.

If there are several note-issuing banks, the exchange of notes against coin and bullion may be avoided by the mutual interchange of notes.

Gray's, London." The object of this clause was chiefly to facilitate the transmission of money, but its effect was to aggravate the difficulties of obtaining small change in the country. *Cf.* the advertisement in the *Newcastle Chronicle* of March 16, 1782, reproduced by Mr. Phillips on the page indicated. The banks then mutually agreed to make their notes payable in the country also, and this constituted a second " optional clause."

Phillips once again hits upon the real cause why notes are presented for conversion : " In 1792 they " (said notes) " became discredited in London, and holders of these notes tried to dispose of them and convert them into coin, the stock of which soon became low in the metropolis and almost exhausted in the country. Then notes were issued for twenty pence, &c., which circulated instead of coin."

Cf. also p. 224, note 2.

[1] To quote one single example, we may point to the history of the City of Glasgow Bank and its failure in 1878.

The jealous competition of the country banks at the close of the eighteenth and at the beginning of the nineteenth century had the effect of limiting the area of circulation of the notes issued by each of them, and caused them either to be refused by the other banks or to be immediately presented for payment in cash at the bank of issue.

All this is obvious. More time is required in gaining sufficient confidence to be entrusted with deposits in account current than in issuing notes and seeing these readily pass into circulation. They pass into circulation almost immediately after the public find that no difficulty is experienced in having the notes cashed. The circulation of the notes will expand as the bank becomes more widely known.

Deposits in account current will not be entrusted to a bank unless the bank forms part of its commercial surroundings, is undetachedly connected with their social conditions, and is one with the customs and habits of the population.[1]

The same rules apply to banks connected with the cheque system.

The holder of a cheque which has been signed for acceptance by the bank on which it is drawn might transfer this document to a third party in the same way as a banknote ; only the acceptance of cheques is not cus-

[1] *Cf.* Bagehot, p. 83 and following.

tomary. A cheque has a short life. If the
bank into which the cheque is paid is the
drawee itself, only the names of its creditors
change. If it be a bank other than the one
upon which the cheque was made out, the
transaction will likewise be neutralised. The
bank which receives the cheque obtains future
capital—a claim on another bank—but gives
at the same time future capital in return, in
the shape of a " deposit," entered in the name
of the depositor of the cheque.

If a cheque be handed to a bank in repayment of a loan or a bill which has fallen due,
one of two things may occur, viz., either future
capital, which the bank possessed, is replaced
by future capital in another form, or, if the
bank exchanges the cheque against another
drawn on itself but which is in the hands of
another banking institution, its loss is counterbalanced by a corresponding diminution of
the future capital issued by itself—that is to
say, by a reduction of its own obligations.

Finally, if a cheque drawn on or a note
issued by a bank be presented for payment in
cash, the bank, by fulfilling its undertaking
to pay, will cancel a liability.

In such a case it receives its own future
capital, which has become present capital, in
return for present capital.

Thus a bank is obliged to keep a certain
amount of present capital in reserve, which,
in case of need, neither distance nor other

circumstances should prevent from being available.

What proportion this reserve should form of a bank's liabilities, experience only can teach. A bank cannot definitely determine in advance the sums which it should retain in short future capital, day to day loans, &c., and neither can it settle *a priori* what amount of present capital it will require.[1]

When a bank grants a cash credit [2] it gives future capital which will be used as and when required.

This corresponds with the granting of a book credit, as long as interest is paid from the time when the funds are actually taken up.

If, on the other hand, the entire loan is paid in notes, a third party will have to give credit by taking over the notes against present

[1] See note 2 on p. 128.

[2] " A cash credit is an undertaking on the part of the bank to advance to an individual such sums of money as he may from time to time require, not exceeding in the whole a certain definite amount ; the individual to whom the credit is given entering into a bond with securities, generally two in number, for the repayment on demand of the sums actually advanced, with interest upon each issue from the day upon which it is made.

" Cash credits are rarely given for sums below £100 ; they generally range from £200 to £500, sometimes reaching £1,000 and occasionally a larger sum.

" A cash credit is, in fact, the same thing as an overdrawn account, except that in a current account the party overdraws on his individual security, and in the cash credit he finds two sureties who are responsible for him." They only exist in Scotland. (Gilbart, ii., p. 223 and following.)

capital. If the public is not prepared to do so, the onus of supplying the demand for present capital will finally devolve upon the bank itself.

It appears from all this, that banks are closely concerned with regularity in the process of production and with the continuous transformation of future into present capital—that is to say, with the repayment of the credit gained by the bank. This has caused some authorities to maintain that since it is obliged to observe a limit a bank can only supply capital if and when its loans are repaid. By them the limit is understood to be a certain proportion between a bank's reserve of present capital and its liabilities. As soon as the proportion between a bank's reserve and its liabilities has reached the figure fixed as the limit, it is no longer in a position to grant further loans, unless and until some of the future capital in its possession has been transformed into present capital.[1]

This cannot be accepted as a hard and fast rule. The process of production does not always follow a regular course. Interruptions occur. If the time occupied in production is too long, a moment will come when present capital is needed to complete the work which has been undertaken. It is then that the bank is called upon to give assistance. But the bank only lends its aid for a short

[1] This doctrine is advocated by Dr. Emil Struck in the pamphlet above referred to, p. 44 and following.

time. The public uses in exchange such balance of its present capital as remains after the amount required for future production has been provided. If this stock is temporarily exhausted, *i.e.*, if no adequate supply is obtainable in such forms as is required by the production of the moment, a bank will feel this by the increase in the number of claims upon it held by its rivals. It must hold counter-claims, or it will be obliged to pay the claims against it in present capital. If it does not hold them, it will curtail its credit facilities, at first to the particular individual in need of capital, afterwards possibly to all borrowers without distinction.

This forms, generally speaking, a bank's limit, viz., the ability of the borrower whose responsibility the bank undertook, to meet his engagements in due course, in connection with the readiness and the power of the community to supply present capital. A bank's reserve, and its proportion to the bank's liabilities, is considered as the barometer of bank management in the same way as the exchanges indicate the movements of international commercial intercourse. This limit is not absolute.[1] In times of panic a bank which issues notes and enjoys public confidence may issue notes and grant book credits liberally. The notes will not be presented for payment in present capital

[1] *Cf.* the practical analysis of this question by George Rae, *The Country Banker*, p. 208 and following.

CONCLUSION 253

nor the book credits withdrawn, as long as they do not reach the bank's rivals. They are merely held by the anxious crowd.

In maintaining this proportion a bank has to observe the following three rules, viz. :

1. That a portion of its liabilities remains permanently in circulation and is never presented for payment in cash.

This is the basis of the Peel Act of 1844. The public cannot spare a certain quantity of circulating medium.

Against this amount the note-issuing bank may hold permanent securities, viz., future capital which is never, or only at the lapse of a great number of years, converted into present capital,[1] provided that it is realisable at any time.

2. That another portion of the future capital issued by a bank—though convertible into cash at any time—is only presented for such payment under special circumstances.

As a rule such special circumstances only

[1] As a rule the English banks hold very little in permanent securities. If in the Banking Returns published by the Joint Stock Banks the share capital, the capital reserve, the notes in circulation (as far as these exist) and " miscellaneous " be added together, a figure is obtained which is approximately equal to the amount of permanent securities. These securities represent about $\frac{4}{15}$ of the total amount of a bank's liabilities. At the same time the cash in hand together with the bills of exchange and advances represent together the same amount as that of the deposits, viz., $\frac{22}{30}$ or $\frac{11}{15}$ of the total liabilities. This is easily understood, since these latter items cover each other.

occur when cash or bullion is required for export abroad. The bank's liabilities remain in circulation for a considerable time, and the bank accepts against them future capital which becomes present capital after not too long an interval.

This makes up that part of a bank's business which grows and diminishes in accordance with the conditions of trade and industry, in which the final results of production are not too long delayed, so that the banks are in a position to take over the future capital (in the case of commercial banks, long future capital) in exchange for their short future capital. Such are the discounts of bills of exchange, the loans for fixed periods, granted to the borrowers and balanced in the bank's books by the deposits, both for fixed periods and at call.

    3. Finally, that a third portion of a bank's liabilities consists of credit operations of very short duration.

This portion is of a fairly regular character, but as its nature is variable a bank holds permanently against it capital " at call," or present capital. It is represented by " day to day " loans, " seven day " loans, money " at call "—balanced on the other side of a bank's account by money in account current and deposits.

These rules show that a bank's credit operations should counterbalance each other, and that they cannot be solely based upon the maintenance of a certain reserve. A bank has to rely upon the conversion into present capital of the future capital which it receives, and the greater the certainty with which the bank may expect this conversion, the greater the confidence with which it will be able to rely upon receiving credit from the public.

A certain amount of present capital should be available :

(1) as cash ;

(2) against emergencies, such as distrust.

In the case of a note-issuing bank this amount must consist of coin or bullion, or both. A purely commercial bank, which does not issue notes, may hold notes and book credits as well as coin and bullion. It is immaterial whether a bank keeps such cash itself or deposits it with a note-issuing bank, of which it uses the fiduciary currency.

In the latter case the note-issuing bank has to be prepared for this liability. It is obliged to keep an adequate amount of circulating medium in its till. For that purpose, however, it may use its own notes. For although, in issuing its own notes, it merely expresses its guarantee in a different way, yet definite payment is effected by them.

The agreement to accept such payment is either consented to by the individual in his acceptance of the note or is declared obligatory by the law.[1]

[1] As a rule this obligation does not apply to the bank itself,

As long as the banknotes have not by special Act been declared inconvertible, they have to be partially covered by a certain amount of present capital, in coin or bullion.

Whilst the Bank of England was not able to adopt a correct attitude with regard to this reserve until the middle of the nineteenth century (though according to its own assertions it was able at any time to meet its engagements and in periods of panic was in a position to do so mainly by the liberal issue of its banknotes), the Act of 1844 restricted its liberty of action in this direction, but placed the covering of banknotes by coin and bullion beyond all doubts. This happened at the very time when the Bank of England itself began to adopt a correct policy with regard to its reserve of coin and bullion.

Thus the Bank of England was limited in its credit operations by the obligation to maintain a fixed quantity of present capital as cover, and the fluctuations therein have acquired a peculiar influence on the English money market. These fluctuations, on account of the close relationship with countries abroad, are greater in London than on any other money market in Europe.

If it is provided that the notes shall not be considered legal tender with regard to the bank of issue itself, the payment—as far as that bank is concerned—depends upon voluntary acceptance by the individual customer.

P. S. KING & SON, WESTMINSTER.

CATALOGUE OF
PUBLICATIONS
ISSUED BY P. S. KING & SON

Africa. Slave Traffic in Portuguese Africa. An Account of Slavery and Slave Trading in Angola and of Slavery in the Islands of San Thome and Principe. By H. R. Fox-Bourne. Demy 8vo. 1s. net. (Inland Postage 1d.)

Africa. *See also* CAPE COLONY; CONGOLAND; EGYPT; *and* SOUTH AFRICA.

Agricultural Labourer. History of the English Agricultural Labourer. By Dr. W. Hasbach. Translated from the German into English. With a Preface by Sidney Webb, LL.B. Demy 8vo. Cloth, 7s. 6d. net. (Inland Postage 5d.)

Agricultural Co-operation. By George Radford, M.A. Royal 8vo. 1s. net. (Inland Postage 2d.)

Agriculture. *See also* BOOKKEEPING; CO-OPERATION; CO-OPERATIVE FARMING; PEOPLE'S BANKS; SMALL HOLDERS; *and* VILLAGE BANKS.

Alcohol. *See* DRINK.

Anti-toxin Serum Treatment. *See* DIPHTHERIA.

Anti-Socialism. *See* NEWÆRA.

Arbitration. Industrial Conciliation and Arbitration. By Douglas Knoop, M.A. With a Preface by Professor S. J. Chapman. Cheap edition, cloth, 3s. 6d. net. (Inland Postage 4d.)

Armaments and War, The Extinction in Perpetuity of. By A. W. Alderson. Demy 8vo. Cloth, 7s. 6d. net. (Inland Postage 3d.)

Assurance. The Assurance Companies Act, 1909. With the Rules and Orders made thereunder by the Board of Trade. With Notes. By Maurice Hawtrey Truelove, of the Inner Temple, Barrister-at-Law. Demy 8vo. 5s. net. (Inland Postage 4d.)

Australia. A Colonial Autocracy. New South Wales under Governor Macquarie, 1810–1821. By Marion Phillips, B.A. (Melbourne), D.Sc. (Econ.), London. (In the Series of the London School of Economics.) Demy 8vo. 10s. 6d. net. (Inland Postage 5d.)

Bank of England, History of. By Professor A. Andréadès. Translated from the French into English. With a Preface by Professor H. S. Foxwell, M.A. Demy 8vo. Cloth, 10s. 6d. net. (Inland Postage 5d.)

Banking. *See* CO-OPERATIVE BANKING ; CO-OPERATIVE CREDIT HANDBOOK ; PEOPLE'S BANKS ; *and* VILLAGE BANKS.

Bibliography of Books on Social and Economic Subjects. *See* WHAT TO READ.

Bibliography of Social Science. The Monthly Journal of the International Institute of Social Bibliography. 2s. net. Annual Subscription, 24s. post free.

This contains the titles of all books dealing with theoretical and practical economics, sociology, and social conditions, the theory and practice of finance, industrial and social statistics, colonial problems, movements of population, and social history ; (2) All the more important articles upon these subjects which appear in periodicals ; (3) The Parliamentary Reports of the chief civilised countries ; (4) Official documents and publications not printed for ordinary circulation, such as the reports and journals of learned societies, commercial institutions, and trade unions, &c.

Up to the present no such bibliography for subjects on social science has been published in England, and it should prove useful to those engaged in political, administrative, or philanthropic work, as well as to all interested in social and economic problems.

[The Publishers will be pleased to send a specimen copy to any address on receipt of the amount of the postage, 2d.]

Bookkeeping. By George Radford, M.A. Reprinted from "Our Land." 3d. net. (Inland postage ½d.)

Boys and Girls, The Early Training of. An Appeal to Working Women. By Ellice Hopkins. This booklet is specially intended for Mothers' Unions. Crown 8vo. 3d. net ; 2s. per dozen. (Inland Postage ½d.)

Brassworkers of Berlin and of Birmingham: A Comparison. Joint Report by R. H. Best, W. J. Davis, and C. Perks, of Birmingham. Fifth Edition. Demy 8vo. 6*d*. net. (Inland Postage 2*d*.) (*See* GERMAN WORKMAN *and* HOW THE ENGLISH WORK-MAN LIVES.)

Building Societies. By Sir Edward Brabrook, C.B., late Chief Registrar of Friendly Societies. A popular treatise advocating the Development and Extension of Building Societies on right lines. Crown 8vo. 1*s*. net. (Inland Postage 2*d*.)

Building Societies. *See also* THRIFT.

Canada. Self-Government in Canada and how it was Achieved : the Story of Lord Durham's Report. By F. Bradshaw, M.A., D.Sc. Demy 8vo. Cloth, 3*s*. 6*d*. net. (Inland Postage 5*d*.)

Canada and the Empire. An Examination of Trade Preferences. By Hon. E. S. Montagu, M.P., and Bron Herbert (Lord Lucas). With a Preface by the Earl of Rosebery, K.G. Crown 8vo. Cloth, 3*s*. 6*d*. net. (Inland Postage 4*d*.)

Canals and Traders. The Argument Pictorial, as applied to the Report of the Royal Commission on Canals and Waterways. By Edwin A. Pratt, author of "British Canals : Is their Resuscitation Possible?" &c. Demy 8vo. 43 Illustrations and Maps. Paper, 1*s*. net. Cloth, 2*s*. 6*d*. net. (Inland Postage 3*d*.)

Cape Colony for the Settler. An Account of its Urban and Rural Industries, their probable Future Development and Extension. By A. R. E. Burton, F.R.G.S. Issued by Order of the Government of the Cape Colony. Demy 8vo. Cloth, with Plates and Map, 2*s*. 6*d*. net. (Inland Postage 5*d*.)

Case-Paper System. *See* POOR LAW.

Catalogue of Parliamentary Papers. *See* PARLIA-MENTARY PAPERS.

Central (Unemployed) Body for London. *See* UNEMPLOYED.

Children's Care Committees. By Margaret Frere. Crown 8vo. 1*s*. net. (Inland Postage 1*d*.)

Children, Legislation in Regard to. Official Report
of the Conference held on May 22 and 23, 1906,
at the Guildhall, London, convened by the British
Section of the International Congress for the Welfare and Protection of Children. Demy 8vo. 1s.
net. (Inland Postage 1d.)

Children. See also BOYS AND GIRLS; INFANT, PARENT,
AND STATE; INFANTILE MORTALITY; PHYSICAL
CONDITION; MEDICAL EXAMINATION OF SCHOOLS
AND SCHOLARS; and UNEMPLOYED.

China Imperial Maritime Customs. Reports on
Trade, Medical Reports, and Reports on Special
Subjects, such as Silk, Opium, Chinese Language,
Music, &c. Issued by Authority of the Inspector-
General of the China Imperial Maritime Customs.
List sent, post free, on application.

China. See also OPIUM.

Colbert. See ECONOMIC POLICY OF COLBERT.

Coal, Foreign Trade in. By H. Stanley Jevons, M.A.,
B.Sc., F.S.S., Lecturer in Economics and Political
Science. (In the Series of the University College
of South Wales and Monmouthshire.) Royal 8vo.
1s. net.

Colonies. See AFRICA; AUSTRALIA; CANADA; and INDIA.

Columbia University, New York. Studies in History,
Economics, and Public Law. Edited by the Faculty
of Political Science at Columbia University. List
of these publications sent, post free, on application.

**Commercial Gambling: Works by Charles William
Smith :—**

"ORIGINAL" THEORIES UPON DEPRES-
SION IN TRADE, AGRICULTURE, AND
SILVER. Price 1s. (Inland Postage 2d.)

COMMERCIAL GAMBLING: the Principal Cause
of Depression in Agriculture and Trade. Price
2s. (Inland Postage 2d.)

THE PRESS ON COMMERCIAL GAMBLING.
Price 6d. (Inland Postage 1d.)

CHARLES W. SMITH'S "REPLY" to the Final Report of the British Royal Commission on Agriculture on the Question of "International Gambling in 'Fictitious' Produce and Silver, under the Option and Future Settlement Systems." Price 2s. (Inland Postage 2d.)

PRICE - FAMINES — THE RESULT OF "CORNERS." The Crime of the Century. Price 1s. (Inland Postage 2d.)

THE TRANSLATED EDITION OF "THE RUIN OF THE WORLD'S AGRICUL-TURE AND TRADE"—"International Fictitious Dealings in Futures of Agricultural Produce and Silver, with their Effect on Prices." By Dr. G. Rühland, of Berlin. Prefaced by C. W. Smith. Price 1s. 6d. (Inland Postage 2d.)

FREE TRADE AND PROTECTION under the International Option and Future Systems, 1846 to 1904. Price 2s. 6d. net. (Inland Postage 4d.)

THE ECONOMIC RUIN OF THE WORLD : International, Commercial, and Financial Gambling in Options and Futures (Marchés à Terme). Price 5s. net. (Inland Postage 4d.)

A MANIFESTO ON INTERNATIONAL, FINAN-CIAL, AND COMMERCIAL GAMBLING in Options and Futures (Marchés à Terme) : The World's Greatest Perils. Price 6d. (Inland Postage 1d.)

A MANIFESTO ON INTERNATIONAL, FINAN-CIAL, AND COMMERCIAL GAMBLING in Options and Futures (Marchés à Terme) in conjunction with Free Trade and Protection. Price 1s. (Inland Postage 1d.)

Commerce. *See* BANK OF ENGLAND; IRELAND; LONDON; LONDON MONEY MARKET; *and* RAILWAYS.

Commons, House of, and Taxation. By Archer Wilde. Demy 8vo. 6d. net. (Inland Postage $\frac{1}{2}d$.)

Communal and Individual Responsibility as Regards Health Conditions. By Mark H. Judge. Reprinted from the *Westminster Review.* Demy 8vo. 6*d.* net. (Inland Postage ½*d.*)

Communal Currency, An Example of. The Facts about the Guernsey Market House. Compiled from original documents. By J. Theodore Harris, B.A. With an Introduction by Sidney Webb, LL.B. (In the Series of the London School of Economics.) Crown 8vo. Paper, 1*s.* net. Cloth, 1*s.* 6*d.* net. (Inland Postage 1½*d.*)

Consols, British, and French Rentes. By C. A. Stanuell. Demy 8vo. 6*d.* net. (Inland Postage 1*d.*)

Co-operation. International Co-operative Bibliography. Compiled and Edited by the Executive Committee of the International Co-operative Alliance. Demy 8vo. Cloth, 7*s.* 6*d.* net. (Inland Postage 4*d.*)

Co-operation. International Co-operative Congress. Report of the Proceedings of the Seventh Congress of the International Co-operative Alliance held at Cremona on September 22–25, 1907. Demy 8vo. 3*s.* net. (Inland Postage 3*d.*)

Co-operation at Home and Abroad. An Account of the Co-operative Movement in Great Britain and other Countries. By C. R. Fay, B.A., D.Sc. Demy 8vo. Cloth, 10*s.* 6*d.* net. (Inland Postage 5*d.*)

Co-operation. *See also* AGRICULTURAL CO-OPERATION; PEOPLE'S BANKS; *and* SMALL HOLDERS.

Co-operative Banking: Its Principles and Practice. With a Chapter on Co-operative Mortgage-Credit. By H. W. Wolff. Demy 8vo. Cloth, 7*s.* 6*d.* net. (Inland Postage 5*d.*)

Co-operative Credit Banks: A help for the Labouring and Cultivating Classes. By H. W. Wolff. Crown 8vo. 6*d.* (Inland Postage 1*d.*)

Co-operative Credit Handbook. By H. W. Wolff. Crown 8vo. 1*s.* net. (Inland Postage 2*d.*)

Co-operative Farming. By W. Bulstrode. A Review of the Causes which have led to the Exodus of the Villagers to the Towns, and a Suggestion for a New Scheme on Commercial Principles. Crown 8vo. 3*d.* net. (Inland Postage ½*d.*)

County Councils. What County Councils can do for the People. By W. Thompson. Demy 8vo, paper, 6*d.* net; cloth, 1*s.* net. (Inland Postage 1*d.*)

Course of Average Prices of General Commodities, 1820–1907. Compiled by Augustus Sauerbeck, F.S.S. Royal 4to. With folding Diagram. 1*s.* net. (Inland Postage 1*d.*)

Danish Poor Relief System. *See* POOR LAW.

Democracy. *See* GERMAN SOCIAL DEMOCRACY ; LIBERALISM ; *and* SOCIAL DEMOCRACY.

Diphtheria. Report of the Bacteriological Diagnosis, and the Anti-Toxin Serum Treatment of cases admitted to the Hospitals of the Metropolitan Asylums Board during the years 1895–6. By G. Sims Woodhead, M.D. Foolscap. 7*s.* 6*d.* net. (Inland Postage 6*d.*)

Drink. Case for Municipal Drink Trade. By Edward R. Pease. Crown 8vo. Cloth, 2*s.* 6*d.* net ; paper, 1*s.* net. (Inland Postage 3*d.*)

Drink. Temperance Reform in the United States. Compiled by A. W. Richardson. With coloured Map. 2*d.* (Inland Postage ½*d.*)

Drink. *See also* NIGERIA.

Economic Policy of Colbert. By A. J. Sargent, M.A. (In the Series of the London School of Economics.) Crown 8vo. Cloth, 2*s.* 6*d.* net. (Inland Postage 3*d.*)

Education. A Short History of National Education in the United Kingdom. By T. Lloyd Humberstone, B.Sc. Demy 8vo. Illustrated. 3*d.* net. (Inland Postage 2*d.*)

*

Education. *See also* BOYS AND GIRLS; CHILDREN'S CARE COMMITTEES; MEDICAL EXAMINATION OF SCHOOLS AND SCHOLARS; *and* PHYSICAL CONDITION OF SCHOOL CHILDREN.

Egypt. The Administration of Justice in Egypt. By H. R. Fox Bourne. Edited, with a Preface, by John M. Robertson, M.P. Demy 8vo, 72 pp. 6*d.* (Inland Postage 1*d.*)

Elections. Practical Notes on the Management of Elections. By Ellis T. Powell, LL.B. (In the Series of the London School of Economics.) Royal 8vo. 1*s.* 6*d.* net. (Inland Postage 2*d.*)

Factory Legislation, History of. By B. L. Hutchins and A. Harrison, D.Sc. With a Preface by Sidney Webb, LL.B. (In the Series of the London School of Economics.) Second edition. Demy 8vo. Cloth, 6*s.* net. (Inland Postage, 4*d.*)

Farming. *See* AGRICULTURE; AGRICULTURAL LABOURER; *and* CO-OPERATIVE FARMING.

Feeble-minded. The Problem of the Feeble-minded. An Abstract of the Report of the Royal Commission on the Care and Control of the Feeble-minded. With an Introduction by Sir Edward Fry, G.C.B., and Contributions by Sir Francis Galton, F.R.S., Rev. W. R. Inge, M.A., Professor A. C. Pigou, and Miss Mary Dendy. Demy 8vo. 1*s.* net. (Inland Postage, 2*d.*)

Finance. *See also* BANKING; CONSOLS; LONDON; MONEY; *and* PUBLIC FINANCE.

Fiscal Fallacies. By Congreve Jackson. Second Edition. Crown 8vo. 3*d.* net. (Inland Postage ½*d.*)

Free Trade. Elements of the Fiscal Problem. By L. G. Chiozza-Money. Demy 8vo. Cloth, 3*s.* 6*d.* net. (Inland Postage 4*d.*)

Free Trade. *See also* BRASSWORKERS; CANADA AND THE EMPIRE; COMMERCIAL GAMBLING; PROTECTION; *and* TARIFFS.

German Social Democracy. Six Lectures delivered at the London School of Economics. By the Hon. Bertrand Russell, B.A. With an Appendix on Social Democracy and Woman's Question in Germany, by Alys Russell, B.A. (In the Series of the London School of Economics.) Crown 8vo. Cloth, 3s. 6d. net. (Inland Postage 3d.)

German Universities. A Review of Professor Paulsen's Work on the German University System. By Mabel Bode, Ph.D. With a Preface and Appendix. Demy 8vo. 1s. net. (Inland Postage 2d.)

German Workman, The: A Study in National Efficiency. By William Harbutt Dawson. A Survey of German Social Legislation and Social Reform Institutions, as they affect the Working-classes. Crown 8vo. Cloth, 6s. net. (Inland Postage 4d.) See BRASS-WORKERS and WORKMEN.

Health. See COMMUNAL; HOUSING; INFANT, PARENT, AND STATE; INFANTILE MORTALITY; MEDICAL EXAMINATION OF SCHOOLS AND SCHOLARS; and SANITARY.

History. Select Documents Illustrating Mediæval and Modern History. A Text Book for use in Colleges and by all Students of History. By Emil Reich. Demy 8vo. Cloth, 21s. net. (Inland Postage 6d.)

History. See also AGRICULTURAL LABOURER; BANK OF ENGLAND; COLUMBIA UNIVERSITY; EDUCATION; FACTORY LEGISLATION; IRELAND; LONDON MUNICIPAL GOVERNMENT; LORDS; PALEOGRAPHY; PHILANTHROPY; POOR LAW; and RATES.

Handbook to the Housing and Town Planning Act, 1909. By W. Thompson, author of "The Housing Handbook," "Housing Up-to-Date," and "What County Councils can do for the People." Demy 8vo, Paper covers, 1s. net. Cloth, 2s. net. (Inland Postage 3d.)

Housing and Town-Planning Act, 1909, The, as it Affects Rural Districts. By Annette Churton. Royal 8vo. 2d. net. (Inland Postage 1d.)

Housing Handbook, Up-to-Date. A Practical Manual for the use of Officers, Members, and Committees of Local Authorities, and Social or Fiscal Reformers. By Alderman W. Thompson. Second edition. Demy 8vo. Cloth. Illustrated, 7s. 6d. net. (Inland Postage 6d.)

Housing. Public Health and Housing. The Influence of the Dwelling upon Health in Relation to the Changing Style of Habitation. Being the Milroy Lectures delivered before the Royal College of Physicians. Revised and Enlarged. By J. F. J. Sykes, M.D., B.Sc. Crown 8vo. Cloth, Diagrams, 5s. net. (Inland Postage 3d.)

India Office and Government of India. List of the more important of these Publications sent post free, on application.

Industrial Conciliation and Arbitration. By Douglas Knoop, M.A. With a Preface by Professor S. J. Chapman. Cloth, 3s. 6d. net (Inland Postage 3d.)

Industrial Conditions. *See* BRASSWORKERS; THE GERMAN WORKMAN; *and* WORKMEN.

Infantile Mortality. Report of the Proceedings of National Conference on Infantile Mortality, held at Caxton Hall, Westminster, on the 13th and 14th June, 1906. Demy 8vo. Limp cloth, 1s. 6d. net. (Inland Postage 3d.)

Infantile Mortality. Report of the Proceedings of the Second National Conference on Infantile Mortality, held at Caxton Hall, Westminster, on the 23rd, 24th, and 25th March, 1908. Demy 8vo. Limp cloth, 1s. 6d. net. (Inland Postage 3d.)

Infantile Mortality and Infants Milk Depôts. By G. F. McCleary, M.D., D.P.H. Illustrated. Crown 8vo. Cloth, 6s. net. (Inland Postage 4d.)

Infant Mortality: Statistical Analysis of, and its Causes in the United Kingdom. By Helen M. Blagg. Demy 8vo. 1s. net. (Inland Postage 1d.)

Infant, Parent, and State. A Social Study and Review. By H. Llewellyn Heath, D P.H. With a Preface by Professor G. Sims Woodhead, M.D. Crown 8vo. Cloth, illustrated, 3s. 6d. net. (Inland Postage 3d.)

Insurance Against Unemployment. By D. F. Schloss. Crown 8vo, cloth, 3s. 6d. net. (Inland Postage 3d.)

Ireland. History of the Commercial and Financial Relations between England and Ireland. By Alice Effie Murray, D.Sc. Preface by W. A. S. Hewins, M.A. (In the Series of the London School of Economics.) Demy 8vo. Cloth, 3s. 6d. net. (Inland Postage 5d.)

Ireland. Paraguay on Shannon : The Price of a Political Priesthood. By F. Hugh O'Donnell, M.A. Demy 8vo, cloth, 6s. net. (Inland Postage 4d.)

Ireland. See also PRICE OF HOME RULE ; and POLITICAL PRIESTS AND IRISH RUIN.

Land, Distribution of. By the Hon. Rollo Russell. Demy 8vo. 3d. net. (Inland Postage 2d.)

Land Values. Rating of Land Values. Notes on the Proposal to levy Rates in respect of Site Values. By Arthur Wilson Fox, C.B. Second edition. Demy 8vo. Cloth, 3s. 6d. net. (Inland Postage 3d.)

Law of Prize on Land and Sea. By Dr. Hans Wehberg, of the University of Bonn. Translated from the German into English. With a Preface by John M. Robertson, M.P. [*In the Press.*

Liberalism. The Crisis of Liberalism. New Issues of Democracy. By J. A. Hobson. Demy 8vo. Cloth. 300 pp. 6s. net. (Inland Postage 4d.)

Licensing. See DRINK.

Light Railways Procedure: Reports and Precedents. Vol. I. By J. Stewart Oxley, M.A., of the Inner Temple, Barrister-at-Law. Demy 8vo. Cloth, 480 pages. 21s. net. (Inland Postage 6d.)

Light Railways Procedure : Reports and Precedents.
Vol. II. By J. Stewart Oxley, M.A., of the Inner
Temple, Barrister-at-Law, assisted by S. W. P.
Beale, B.A., of Lincoln's Inn, Barrister-at-Law.
Demy 8vo, cloth, 376 pages. 21s. net. (Inland
Postage 5d.)

Liquor Traffic. *See* DRINK ; *and* NIGERIA.

Local Government. *See* COMMUNAL CURRENCY; HOUS-
ING; LONDON MUNICIPAL GOVERNMENT ; NATIONAL
AND LOCAL FINANCE ; POOR LAW ; TAXATION ; *and*
TOWN PLANNING.

Local Taxation in London. *See* LONDON.

**London Building Act, Tribunal of Appeal under
the.** A Manual for Appellants. By Charles H.
Love. Demy 8vo. Cloth, 3s. 6d. net. (Inland
Postage 3d.)

London County Council. Messrs. P. S. King & Son
are the publishers appointed for the sale of the
reports and publications of the London County
Council. Special catalogue, arranged under subjects, post free on application.

London Municipal Government. The History of a
Great Reform, 1880–1888. By John Lloyd, Hon.
Secretary and Secretary of the Municipal Reform
League. Large quarto, 72 pp., 21 illustrations,
handsomely bound in half blue calf. Special
edition limited to 200 copies. Price £1 1s. net.
(Inland Postage 5d.)

London. Local Taxation in London. By M. E. Lange.
With a Preface by Lord Welby. Demy 8vo. 1s.
net. (Inland Postage 1½d.)

London : Mechanism of the City. An Analytical Survey
of the Business Activities of the City of London.
By Ellis T. Powell, LL.B. (Lond.), B.Sc., of the
Inner Temple, Barrister-at-Law.   [*In the Press.*

London Pride and London Shame. By L. Cope Cornford. Demy 8vo. Cloth, 6s. net. (Inland Postage 4d.)

Lords, House of, and Taxation. By Ernest E. Williams. Demy 8vo. 6d. net. (Inland Postage ½d.)

Lords, The. Their History and Powers, with Special Reference to Money Bills and the Veto. By Adrian Wontner, of Gray's Inn, Barrister-at-Law. Crown 8vo. 1s. net. (Inland Postage 2d.)

Lords. *See also* SUPREME SENATE.

Machine Drawing. A Text-book for Students preparing for Science Examinations in Technical and Evening Schools. By Alfred P. Hill. Demy 4to. Limp cloth, 2s. 6d. net. (Inland Postage 3d.)

Medical Examination of Schools and Scholars. A Manual for School Doctors and Educationalists. A Symposium of Experts. Edited by T. N. Kelynack, M.D. Demy 8vo. Cloth, 10s. 6d. net. (Inland Postage 6d.)

Money. A Corner in Gold and our Money Laws. An Argument against the Main Defects of our Money System. With a reprint of the speeches of the Right Hon. Sir Robert Peel, Bart., in the House of Commons, 1844, on the Renewal of the Bank Charter and the State of the Law affecting Currency and Banking. Crown 8vo. Cloth, 2s. 6d. net.

Money. The Rise of the London Money Market, 1640–1826. By W. Roosegaarde Bisschop, LL.D. With an Introduction by Prof. H. S. Foxwell, M.A. Crown 8vo. 5s. net. (Inland Postage 4d.)

Mothers' Unions. *See* BOYS AND GIRLS.

Motor Traction. The Locomotion Problem. By Charles Bright, F.R.S.E., M.I.E.E. Demy 8vo. 1s. net. (Inland Postage 1½d.)

Municipal Manual. A Description of the Constitution and Functions of Urban Local Authorities. By A. E. Lauder. Crown 8vo, 3s. 6d. net. (Inland Postage 4d.)

Municipal. *See also* DRINK ; HOUSING ; RATES ; TAXATION ; *and* TOWN PLANNING.

National and Local Finance. A Review of the Relations between the Central and Local Authorities in England, France, Belgium, and Prussia during the Nineteenth Century. By J. Watson Grice, B.Sc. With a preface by Sidney Webb, LL.B. (In the Series of the London School of Economics). Demy 8vo. Cloth, 10s. 6d. net. (Inland Postage 5d.)

Nationalisation of Railways. *See* RAILWAYS.

Newæra. A Socialist Romance, with a Chapter on Vaccination. By EDWARD G. HERBERT, B.Sc. Demy 8vo. 6s. net. (Inland Postage 4d.)

Nigeria, Liquor Traffic in Southern. As set forth in the Report of the Government Committee of Inquiry, 1909. An Examination and a Reply. Published for the Native Races and the Liquor Traffic United Committee. Royal 8vo, 3d. net. (Inland Postage 1½d.)

Opium: International Opium Commission, Shanghai, February, 1909. Complete Official Report of Proceedings and Reports of Delegations. In 2 Vols. Volume I.—Report and Minutes of Proceedings. Volume II.—Reports of Delegations. F'cap. folio. About 500 pp. As containing the Findings of the Commission and the complete Reports of all the Delegations, these Volumes will be indispensable to all students of the subject. Price 10s. net. (Inland Postage 6d.)

Paleography. Pipe Roll of the Bishopric of Winchester. From the Fourth Year of the Episcopate of Peter des Roches, A.D. 1207–1208. By the Class in Paleography at the London School of Economics, under the supervision of Hubert Hall, F.S.A. (In the Series of the London School of Economics.) F'cap folio, 15s. net. (Inland Postage 5d.)

Parliamentary Papers, 1801–1900, Catalogue of. A General Catalogue of the principal Reports and Papers published during the nineteenth century—also a few of earlier date—with prices, and in most cases analyses of contents. Printed with wide margins for convenience of librarians and others wishing to make notes, shelf, or reference numbers, &c. Medium 4to. Full buckram, 7s. 6d. net. (Inland Postage 6d.)

Parliamentary Papers, Monthly Catalogue of. Post free on application.

Peace. *See* WAR.

People's Banks: A Record of Social and Economic Success. By H. W. Wolff, author of "Co-operative Banking," "Agricultural Banks," &c. Third Edition, Revised and Enlarged. Demy 8vo. Cloth, 600 pages. 6s. net. (Inland Postage 6d.)

Philanthropy. History of English Philanthropy, from the Dissolution of the Monasteries to the taking of the First Census. By B. Kirkman Gray. Demy 8vo. Cloth, 7s. 6d. net. (Inland Postage 4d.)

Philanthropy. Philanthropy and the State, or Social Politics. By B. Kirkman Gray. Edited by Eleanor Kirkman Gray and B. L. Hutchins. A companion volume to "History of English Philanthropy," by the same author. Demy 8vo. Cloth, 7s. 6d. net. (Inland Postage 5d.)

Physical Condition of School Children. Report on the Physical Condition of 1,400 School Children in the City of Edinburgh, together with some Account of their Homes and Surroundings. Prepared by a Committee of Edinburgh Citizens, and published for the Edinburgh Charity Organisation Society. Royal 4to, 5s. net. (Inland Postage, 5d.)

Political Priests and Irish Ruin. By F. H. O'Donnell, M.A., author of "A History of the Irish Parliamentary Party." A Second Edition, revised and brought up to date, of the author's previous work "Paraguay on Shannon." Demy 8vo. 1s. net. (Inland Postage 3d.)

Political Socialism: A Remonstrance. A Collection of Papers by Members of the British Constitution Association, with Presidential Addresses by Lord Balfour of Burleigh and Lord Hugh Cecil. Edited by Mark H. Judge. Crown 8vo. Paper boards, 1s. net; cloth, 1s. 6d. net. (Inland Postage 3d.)

Poor Law. Administrative Reform and the Local Government Board. By J. Theodore Dodd, M.A. Crown 8vo. 1s. 6d. net. (Inland Postage 2d.)

Poor Law. The English Poor Laws: their History, Principles, and Administration. Three Lectures delivered at the Women's University Settlement, Southwark. By Sophia Lonsdale. Third and revised edition. Crown 8vo. 1s. net. (Inland Postage 2d.)

Poor Law. The Danish Poor Relief System: an Example for England. By Edith Sellers. An account of the Poor Relief System as practised in Denmark, which is generally considered to be a model of its kind. Crown 8vo. Limp cloth, 2s. net. (Inland Postage 2d.)

Poor Law. Glimpses into the Abyss. By Mary Higgs. An account of the personal explorations undertaken by Mrs. Higgs, who, disguised as a tramp, has spent days and nights in tramp-wards, lodging-houses, and shelters. Crown 8vo. Cloth, 3s. 6d. net. (Inland Postage 4d.)

Poor Law. History of the English Poor Law, 924–1853. In connection with the legislation and other circumstances affecting the condition of the people. By Sir George Nicholls, K.C.B. Revised edition, with a Biography and Portrait of the Author. 2 vols. Demy 8vo. Cloth, 10s. 6d. net. (Inland Postage 7d.)

Poor Law. History of the English Poor Law, 1834–1898, By Thomas Mackay. Demy 8vo. Cloth, 7s. 6d. net. (Inland Postage 6d.)

Poor Law. The History Sheet or Case-Paper System. A collection of Papers read at various Poor Law Conferences, with the Discussions thereon and Specimen Forms in use in various Unions. With an Introduction by Sir William Chance, Bart. Crown 8vo. Cloth back, 2s. net. (Inland Postage 3d.)

Poor Law. Memorandum on the Reports of the Royal Commission on the Poor Laws. By Sir Arthur Downes. Demy 8vo. 2d. net. (Inland Postage ½d.)

Poor Law. Memorandum on the Reports of the Royal Commission on the Poor Laws. By Miss Octavia Hill. 1d. 7s. 6d. per 100 copies. (Inland Postage ½d.)

Poor Law. Our Treatment of the Poor. By Sir William Chance, Bart., M.A. Crown 8vo. Cloth, 2s. 6d. (Inland Postage 3d.)

Poor Law : The Poor and Their Rights. How to Obtain them Under Existing Legislation. By J. Theodore Dodd, M.A., Guardian and Councillor for the City of Oxford. Demy 8vo. 6d. net. (Inland Postage 1d.)

Poor Law : Poor Law Reform, viâ Tertia. The Case for the Guardians. By Sir William Chance, Bart., M.A. Crown 8vo. 1s. net. Cloth, 1s. 6d. net. (Inland Postage 3d.)

Poor Law. The Starting Point of Poor Law Reform. The Principles in Common, and at issue, in the Reports of the Poor Law Commission. By John H. Muirhead, M.A., LL.D. With an Introduction by Sir Oliver Lodge, LL.D., F.R.S. Second Edition. Demy 8vo. Cloth back, 2s. net. (Inland Postage 3d.)

Poor Law. See also VAGRANCY.

Poor Law Conferences. Official Reports of the Proceedings of the Central and District Poor Law Conferences, containing the Papers read and the full Discussions thereon. Report of any single Conference, 1s.; all Conferences, each sent as soon as published, 10s. 6d. per annum ; Bound Volume, with index, 12s. net. (Inland Postage 5d.)

Poor Law Orders. Arranged and Annotated by H. Jenner-Fust, M.A. Second edition. Royal 8vo. 42s. net. (Inland Postage 6d.)

Poverty, Causes of. By Callaghan McCarthy, B.A. A graphic description of the parts and appearances of this planet—of its surface, its instruments of production, the items of property, its vegetable and animal life, its human communities, &c. The author brings all these vividly before the reader's mind, and explains the defects that give rise to human poverty. Crown 8vo. Cloth, 2s. net. (Inland Postage 2½d.)

Practical Notes on the Management of Elections. By Ellis T. Powell, LL.B. (In the Series of the London School of Economics.) Demy 8vo. Paper, 1s. 6d. net. (Inland Postage 1½d.)

Price of Home Rule, The. By L. Cope Cornford. Crown 8vo. Cloth, 1s. net. Paper, 6d. net. (Inland Postage 1d.)

Prices. Course of Average Prices of General Commodities, 1820–1907. Compiled by Augustus Sauerbeck, F.S.S. Royal 4to. With folding Diagram. 1s. net. (Inland Postage 1d.)

Production and Distribution. A History of the Theories of Production and Distribution in English Political Economy from 1776–1848. By Edwin Cannan, M.A., LL.D. Second edition. Demy 8vo. Cloth, 10s. 6d. net. (Inland Postage 5d.)

Progress: Civil, Social, and Industrial. The Quarterly Magazine of the British Institute of Social Service. 6d. net. (Inland Postage 2d.)

Contains the Official Record of the National League for Physical Education and Improvement, and information regarding Foreign Social Activities, by Dr. Rodolphe Broda. A full list of all Publications on Social Topics, including Articles in Periodicals during the preceding quarter, forms an invaluable feature of each issue.

The Publishers will be pleased to send a specimen copy to any address on receipt of the amount of the postage.

Protection in Canada and Australasia. By C. H. Chomley, B.A., LL.B. Crown 8vo. Cloth, 3*s*. 6*d*. net. (Inland Postage 3*d*.)

Protection in France. By H. O. Meredith, M.A. Crown 8vo. Cloth, 3*s*. 6*d*. net. (Inland Postage 3*d*.)

Protection in Germany. A History of German Fiscal Policy during the Nineteenth Century. By William Harbutt Dawson. Crown 8vo. Cloth, 3*s*. 6*d*. net. (Inland Postage 4*d*.)

Protection in the United States. A study of the origin and growth of the American Tariff System and its social and economic influences. By. A. Maurice Low. Crown 8vo. Cloth, 3*s*. 6*d*. net. (Inland Postage 3*d*.)

Protection. *See also* CANADA AND THE EMPIRE; COMMERCIAL GAMBLING; FISCAL FALLACIES; FREE TRADE; SEVEN YEARS OF THE SUGAR CONVENTION; TARIFFS; *and* TARIFF REFORM.

Public Finance. The King's Revenue. An account of the Revenue and Taxes raised in the United Kingdom, with a short history of each Tax and Branch of the Revenue. By W. M. J. Williams. Demy 8vo. Cloth, 6*s*. net. (Inland Postage 4*d*.)

Railways: The Railway Clerk's Assistant. By Geo. B. Lissenden. Crown 8vo. 1*s*. 6*d*. net. (Inland Postage 3*d*.)

Railway Trader's Guide, The. The Railway Trader's Guide to Forwarding, Receiving, Railway Charges, and all other Matters incidental to Transactions with the Railway Companies. By Geo. B. Lissenden. Royal 8vo. Cloth. 250 pp., including 48 pp. of Ready Reckoner, in addition to other tables and specimen forms. 7*s*. 6*d* net. (Inland Postage 5*d*.)

Railways. Monthly Bulletin of the International Railway Congress (English edition). Illustrated. Single numbers vary in price from 2*s*. to 6*s*. each. Subscription for 12 months, Jan.–Dec. only 24*s*.

Railways. Railways and Nationalisation. By Edwin A. Pratt. Crown 8vo. Cloth, 2s. 6d. net. (Inland Postage 4d.)

Railways. The Safety of British Railways; or Railway Accidents, how caused, and how prevented. By H. Raynar Wilson. Crown 8vo. Cloth, 3s. 6d. net. (Inland Postage 3d.)

Railways. See also LIGHT RAILWAYS.

Rates. History of Local Rates in England. By Edwin Cannan, M.A. A summary of the Development of one element of taxation. (In the Series of the London School of Economics.) Crown 8vo. Cloth, 2s. 6d. net. (Inland Postage 3d.)

Rates. Being the Revenue and Expenditure of Boroughs and Urban District Councils of 10,000 or more inhabitants (England and Wales) analysed and compared. By C. Ashmore Baker, A.M.I.E.E. F'cap. folio. Paper boards. 2s. 6d. net. (Inland Postage 4d.)

Rates. See also LONDON ; MUNICIPAL ; NATIONAL AND LOCAL FINANCE ; and TAXATION AND LOCAL GOVERNMENT.

Rating and Assessment in London. Quinquennial Valuation, 1910. A Guide for Officials and Rate-payers. With information as to the Principles upon which the Valuation is made, and as to how the Valuation is tested and in a Proper case reduced or otherwise adjusted. By Edwin Austin, of Gray's Inn, Barrister-at-Law. Crown 8vo. Cloth, 2s. net. Paper, 1s. net. (Inland Postage 2d.)

Rating of Land Values. See LAND VALUES.

Referendum. See LIBERALISM ; and SWITZERLAND.

Sanitary Inspector's Guide. A Practical Treatise on the Public Health Act, 1875, and the Public Health Acts Amendment Act, 1890, so far as they affect the Inspector of Nuisances. By H. Lemmoin-Cannon. Crown 8vo. Cloth, 3s. 6d. net. (Inland Postage 3d.)

Schools, Medical Examination of. *See* MEDICAL.

Second Chamber. *See* LIBERALISM ; LORDS ; *and* SUPREME SENATE.

Seven Years of the Sugar Convention : 1903-1910. A Vindication of Mr. Chamberlain's Imperial and Commercial Policy. By Ralph T. Hinckes, M.A. Crown 8vo. 3*d.* net. (Inland Postage 1*d.*)

Sewage Works Analyses. An account of the methods of analysis in use in the laboratory of the Manchester Corporation sewage works. By Gilbert J. Fowler, F.I.C. Crown 8vo. Cloth, illustrated, 6s. net. (Inland Postage 4*d.*)

Site Values. *See* LAND VALUES.

Small Holders : What they must do to succeed. With a chapter on the revival of country life. By Edwin A. Pratt. Crown 8vo. Cloth back, 2*s.* net. (Inland Postage 3*d.*)

Small Holdings. The Small Holdings Controversy. Ownership *v.* Tenancy. By Mrs. Roland Wilkins (L. Jebb). With a Prefatory Letter by Lord Carrington. Demy 8vo. 2*d.* net. (Inland Postage ½*d.*)

Small Holdings in England. By Frederick Impey. Demy 8vo. 3*d.* net. (Inland Postage, 1*d.*)

Social Democracy, New. A Study for the Times. By J. H. Harley, M.A., late Scholar of Mansfield College, Oxford ; Vice-President of the National Union of Journalists. Demy 8vo. Cloth, 6*s.* net. (Inland Postage 4*d.*)

Social Democracy. *See also* GERMAN SOCIAL DEMOCRACY ; *and* LIBERALISM.

Socialism : Newæra : A Socialist Romance, with a Chapter on Vaccination. By Edward G. Herbert, B.Sc. Demy 8vo. 6*s.* net. (Inland Postage 4*d.*)

Socialism. *See also* GERMAN SOCIAL DEMOCRACY ; LIBERALISM ; SOCIAL DEMOCRACY ; *and* POLITICAL SOCIALISM.

Spencer. Herbert Spencer Refutes recent Misrepresenta-
tions. Professor Bourne's defamatory attacks met
by excerpts culled from the Philosopher's works.
By Alfred W. Tillett. Crown 8vo. 6*d.* net. (Inland Postage ½*d.*)

State Railways. *See* RAILWAYS.

Statistics, An Elementary Manual of. By Arthur L.
Bowley, M.A., F.S.S., Reader in Statistics in the
University of London. Author of "Elements of
Statistics," &c. Demy 8vo. Cloth, 5*s.* net. (In-
land Postage 4*d.*)

Statistics, Elements of. A Text Book for the use of
students, actuaries, bankers, &c. By A. L. Bowley,
M.A. Third and revised edition. (In the Series of
the London School of Economics.) Demy 8vo.
Cloth. Numerous Diagrams. 10*s.* 6*d.* net. (Inland Postage 5*d.*)

Supreme Senate and a Strong Empire, A. By R. V.
Wynne. F'cap. 8vo. 6*d.* net. (Inland Postage ½*d.*)

Switzerland, Referendum in. By M. Simon Deploige.
With a letter on the Referendum in Belgium by
M. J. van den Heuvel. Translated by C. P.
Trevelyan, M.P., and edited with notes, introduc-
tion, bibliography and appendices by Lilian Tomn.
(In the Series of the London School of Economics.)
Crown 8vo. Cloth, 7*s.* 6*d.* net. (Inland Postage 4*d.*)

Tariff Reform. The Manufacturer and the State. An
Address by H. Hirst, M.I.E.E. Demy 8vo. 6*d.* net.
(Inland Postage 1*d.*)

Tariff Reform. Fiscal Fallacies: A Comparison with
Germany. By Congreve Jackson. Second Edition.
Crown 8vo. 3*d.* net. (Inland Postage 1*d.*)

Tariff Reform, The Real Case for. Employment and
Wages — How Free Trade "Blacklegs" Home
Labour—Facts for Workmen by a Workman (T.
Good). With a Preface by the Rt. Hon. J. Austen
Chamberlain, M.P. Demy 8vo. 6*d.* net. (Inland
Postage 1*d.*)

Tariffs. Statistical Studies Relating to National Progress in Wealth and Trade since 1882 : A plea for further inquiry. By Arthur L. Bowley, M.A. Crown 8vo. 2s. net. (Inland Postage 2d.)

Tariffs. Tariff Commission Report. List of the volumes containing Report and Summary of Evidence, Evidence of Witnesses, Replies to Forms, Tables, and Diagrams Dealing with Iron, Steel, Textile, Agriculture, Engineering, Pottery, Glass, Sugar and Confectionery, post free on application.

Tariffs. The Tariff Problem. By Professor W. J. Ashley. Second Edition. Crown 8vo. Cloth, 3s. 6d. net. (Inland Postage 4d.)

Tariffs. *See also* CANADA AND THE EMPIRE; COMMERCIAL GAMBLING; FREE TRADE; *and* PROTECTION.

Taxation. *See* COMMONS; FREE TRADE; LORDS; NATIONAL AND LOCAL FINANCE; PROTECTION; PUBLIC FINANCE; *and* TAXATION AND LOCAL GOVERNMENT.

Taxation and Local Government. By J. C. Graham. Fourth Edition, revised and brought up-to-date. By M. D. Warmington. Crown 8vo. Cloth, 2s. net. (Inland Postage 3d.)

Temperance. *See* DRINK.

Thrift, Approved Methods of. With a list of societies for its promotion. By Mrs. A. H. Johnson. Issued for the National Union of Women Workers of Great Britain and Ireland. Demy 8vo. 3d. net. (Inland Postage ½d.)

Thrift, Institutions for. By Sir Edward Brabrook, C.B., F.S.A. A useful little book for members of working men's clubs, friendly societies, building societies and other institutions of a similar nature. Crown 8vo. 6d. net. (Inland Postage 1d.)

Thrift Manual. A Manual on Thrift for the use of Teachers in Primary Schools. Demy 8vo. Limp cloth, 2s. net. (Inland Postage 2½d.)

Thrift. *See also* BUILDING SOCIETIES.

Town Planning Powers. The Practical Application of Town Planning Powers. Report of a National Town Planning Conference arranged by the Garden Cities and Town Planning Association, held at the Guildhall, London, on December 10, 1909. Papers and Speeches by Thomas Adams, J. W. Willis Bund, K.C., W. R. Davidge, H. V. Lanchester, A. R. Stenning, H. Inigo Triggs, Raymond Unwin, Paul Waterhouse, and Professors S. D. Adshead, Patrick Geddes, and Beresford Pite. Edited by Ewart G. Culpin. Demy 8vo. 1s. net. (Inland Postage 2½d.)

Town Planning. *See also* HOUSING.

Trade Unions. Select Documents Illustrating the History of Trade Unionism. [1. The Tailoring Trade.] By F. W. Galton. With a Preface by Sidney Webb, LL.B. Crown 8vo. Cloth, 5s. net. (Inland Postage 4d.)

Tramps. *See* POOR LAW; UNEMPLOYED; VAGRANCY; *and* WHERE SHALL SHE LIVE?

Transport Facilities in the Mining and Industrial Districts of South Wales and Monmouthshire. Their future History and Development. By Clarence S. Howells, M.A. No. 2 of the Series of Publications of the Department of Economics and Political Science of the University College of South Wales and Monmouthshire. Edited by H. Stanley Jevons, M.A., B.Sc. 2s. net. (Inland Postage 1½d.)

Unemployed : Central Body for London. Preliminary Report on the work of the Central (Unemployed) Body for London to May 12, 1906. Foolscap 1s. net. (Inland Postage 2d.)
   Second Report from May 12, 1906, to June 30, 1907. Foolscap. 1s. net. (Inland Postage 5d.)
   Third Report of the Central Body, from July 1, 1907, to June 30, 1909. F'cap. 1s. 6d. net. (Inland Postage 5d.)

Unemployed. Insurance Against Unemployment. By David F. Schloss. Crown 8vo. Cloth, 3s. 6d. net. (Inland Postage 3d.)

Unemployed. The Labour Exchange in Relation to Boy and Girl Labour. By Frederick Keeling. Demy 8vo. 6d. net. (Inland Postage 1½d.)

Unemployed. Report of a Temporary Colony at Garden City for Unemployed Workmen mainly from West Ham during February, March and April, 1905. Carried out by the Trinity College (Oxford) Settlement, Stratford, London. Demy 8vo. 6d. net. (Inland Postage ½d.)

Unemployed. The Unemployables. By Edmond Kelly, M.A. With a Preface by Sir William Chance, Bart., M.A. Contains a full account of the Swiss Labour Colonies in the Canton of Berne. Crown 8vo. 6d. net. (Inland Postage 1d.)

Unemployed. The Unemployed : a National Question. By Percy Alden, M.A. With a Preface by Sir John Gorst, M.A. Second edition. Crown 8vo. Cloth, 2s. net. (Inland Postage 3d.)

Unemployment and the Unemployed. A Bibliography. Prepared by F. Isabel Taylor, B.Sc., Formerly Senior Student-Assistant in the Library of the London School of Economics. With a Preface by Sidney Webb, LL.B. (In the Series of the London School of Economics.) Demy 8vo. Cloth, 2s. net. Paper, 1s. 6d. net. (Inland Postage 2d.)

Unemployment. The Sun's Heat and Trade Activity as a Cause of Unemployment. By H. Stanley Jevons, M.A., B.Sc., F.S.S. Royal 8vo. Cloth, 2s. net. Paper, 1s. net. (Inland Postage, 2d.)

Vaccination and Vivisection. Politics and Disease. By A. Goff and J. H. Levy. Crown 8vo. Cloth, 3s. 6d. net. (Inland Postage 4d.)

Vagrancy. A Review of the Report of the Departmental Committee on Vagrancy, 1906. With answers to certain criticisms. By Sir William Chance, Bart., M.A. Crown 8vo. 6d. net. (Inland Postage, 1d.)

Vagrancy. A Vicar as Vagrant. By Rev. G. Z. Edwards. With a Preface by the Rector of Birmingham. Demy 8vo. 2*d*. (Inland Postage ½*d*.)

Vagrancy Problem, The. The Case for Measures of Restraint for Vagrants, Loafers, and Unemployables; with a Study of Continental Detention Colonies and Labour Houses. By William Harbutt Dawson, author of "The German Workman." Crown 8vo. 5*s*. net. (Inland Postage 4*d*.)

Village Banks. How to Start them; How to Work them; What the Rich may do to Help them, &c. By H. W. Wolff. Crown 8vo. 6*d*. (Inland Postage ½*d*.)

Vagrancy. *See also* POOR LAW; UNEMPLOYED; *and* WHERE SHALL SHE LIVE?

War. The Extinction in Perpetuity of Armaments and War. By A. W. Alderson. Demy 8vo. Cloth, 7*s*. 6*d*. net. (Inland Postage 3*d*.)

War. *See also* LAW OF PRIZE.

What County Councils can do for the People. By W. Thompson. Demy 8vo; paper, 6*d*.; cloth, 1*s*. (Inland Postage 1*d*.)

What to Read on Social and Economic Subjects. An Interleaved Bibliography. Fifth Edition. Demy 8vo. 1*s*. net. (Inland Postage 3*d*.)

Where Shall She Live? The Homelessness of the Woman Worker. Written for the National Association for Women's Lodging Homes. By Mary Higgs and Edward E. Hayward, M.A. Crown 8vo. Cloth, 2*s*. 6*d*. net. Paper, 1*s*. 6*d*. net. (Inland Postage 3*d*.)

Women. Educated Working Women. The Economic Position of Women Workers in the Middle Classes. By Clara E. Collet, M.A. Crown 8vo. Cloth, 2*s*. 6*d*. net; paper, 2*s*. net. (Inland Postage, 3*d*.)

Women. Women as Barmaids. Published for the Joint Committee on the Employment of Barmaids. With an Introduction by the Bishop of Southwark. Demy 8vo. 1*s*. net. (Inland Postage 1½*d*.)

Women. Women in the Printing Trades : A Sociological Study. Edited by J. R. Macdonald, M.P. With a Preface by Professor F. Y. Edgeworth. Demy 8vo. Cloth. Diagrams. 10s. 6d. net. (Inland Postage 4d.)

Workmen. How the English Workman Lives : Being the Experiences of a German Coal-miner in England. Translated by C. H. d'E. Leppington. Crown 8vo. 1s. net. (*See* BRASSWORKERS ; *and* GERMAN WORK-MAN.)